A.A. Castor

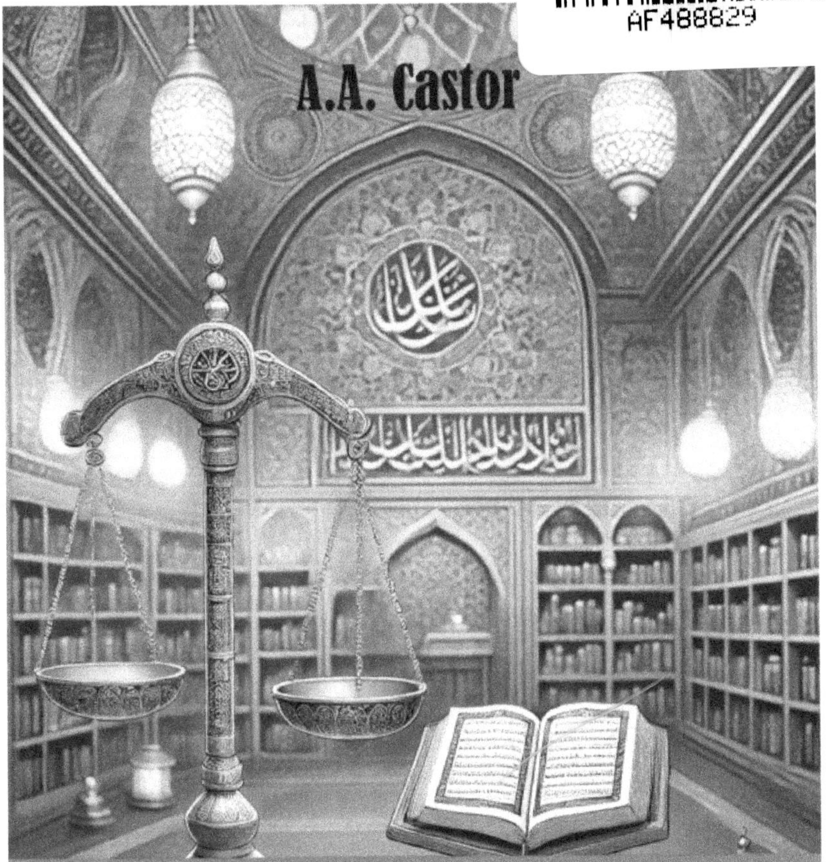

Governance Through Justice

What Today's Leaders Can Learn from Omar ibn al-Khattab

Table of Contents

Governance Through Justice: What Today's Leaders Can Learn from Omar ibn al-Khattab

A.A. Castor

A.A. Castor

Dedication

To my beloved family,

Your unconditional love, unwavering support, and endless encouragement have been my greatest blessings. From the earliest days of dreaming to the challenging moments of writing, you have stood by me with patience and belief. This book is as much yours as it is mine, a reflection of the values you've instilled and the faith you've shown in me. Thank you for being my rock and my inspiration.

To my dear friends,

Your friendship has illuminated my path with laughter, shared moments, and invaluable support. You've cheered me on through every triumph and lifted me up through every challenge. Your belief in my endeavors has been a source of strength and motivation. This book is a testament to the power of friendship, and I am grateful for each of you who has walked this journey by my side.

To God,

Your grace and guidance have been my constant companions. In moments of doubt, you've shown me the way; in moments of joy, you've multiplied my gratitude. This book is a testament to your faithfulness and the blessings you've bestowed upon me. May it serve as a reflection of your love and the lessons you continue to teach me.

With heartfelt gratitude and love,

A.A. Castor

Copyright © 2024 by A.A. Castor

---

1. http://www.tonyc.info

Why I Am Writing This Book

The legacy of Omar ibn al-Khattab (may Allah be pleased with him) has resonated through centuries, providing a timeless example of ethical, just, and visionary leadership. As I reflect on the challenges that modern leaders face today—rising inequality, political divisions, moral crises, and the erosion of trust in leadership—I am increasingly drawn to the profound lessons we can learn from history. Omar's life offers a blueprint for navigating these complex issues with integrity, humility, and courage. This book is my attempt to bring those lessons to the forefront, not just as a historical study, but as a guide for modern leaders who seek to govern with justice and compassion.

In a world where power is often synonymous with personal gain, and leadership is frequently disconnected from the people it serves, Omar's approach to governance offers an antidote. His unwavering commitment to justice, his refusal to elevate himself above the law, and his deep empathy for the vulnerable remind us of the qualities that define true leadership. I believe that these principles are not relics of the past but are urgently needed today. Whether in politics, business, or community organizations, leaders must reconnect with the values that Omar exemplified—justice, humility, accountability, and a deep concern for the well-being of others.

The idea for this book came as I observed a growing dissatisfaction with leadership in our time. There is a yearning for leaders who are not only effective but also morally grounded, who make decisions not for short-term gains but for the long-term welfare of the people they serve. Omar's leadership embodies these traits. His ability to balance strength with compassion, decisiveness with humility, and justice with mercy is something I believe the world needs more of today. I am writing this book because I believe Omar's example can inspire a new generation of leaders to lead with integrity, to value the welfare of their communities, and to govern with a vision that extends beyond personal success.

This book is not just about history; it's about the future. By studying the life of Omar ibn al-Khattab, we can rediscover the essence of ethical leadership, which is so critical to building just, fair, and prosperous societies. My hope is that this book will serve as both a tribute to one of history's greatest leaders and a practical guide for those who seek to lead with the same courage, wisdom, and integrity that Omar demonstrated. This is why I am writing this book—to remind us of the timeless principles that should guide every leader and to inspire a new generation of leadership grounded in justice, humility, and service to humanity.

Warning and Disclaimer

The author and publisher of this book have made every effort to ensure the accuracy of the information contained within. However, the content provided is for informational and educational purposes only and is not intended as professional advice. Readers are encouraged to consult appropriate professionals or experts before making decisions based on the material presented in this book.

The author and publisher assume no responsibility or liability for any errors, omissions, or outcomes related to the use of the information provided. Under no circumstances will the author or publisher be held liable for any direct, indirect, incidental, or consequential damages resulting from the use of, or reliance on, the material contained in this book.

All content is provided "as is" without any warranties of any kind, express or implied. The reader assumes full responsibility for the application of any ideas or strategies discussed herein.

By reading this book, you agree to hold the author and publisher harmless from any claims, actions, or damages resulting from your interpretation or use of the information presented.

About the Author

A.A. Castor is a dedicated writer, researcher, and historian with a deep passion for exploring the intersections of history, leadership, and social philosophy. His work spans a wide range of topics, from political strategy and governance to religious history and ethical leadership. With a focus on uncovering timeless lessons from the past and applying them to contemporary challenges, Castor aims to provide practical insights for both personal and professional development.

A Filipino historian, Castor draws inspiration from historical figures such as Omar ibn al-Khattab, Augustus Caesar, and Salah ad-Din Yusuf ibn Ayyub, whose leadership qualities and moral integrity continue to inspire him. Through his writings, Castor explores the lives of these great leaders, offering a blend of historical study, leadership theory, and philosophical reflection.

In addition to his research, Castor is an avid podcaster and speaker, engaging his audience on topics related to leadership, history, and social dynamics. His podcast series delves into the lessons that historical figures can teach us about navigating modern-day leadership challenges with courage, wisdom, and compassion.

A.A. Castor continues to write extensively on leadership, history, and religious philosophy, aiming to inspire current and future leaders to embrace values of justice, humility, and empathy in their work and lives.

The Legacy of Omar ibn al-Khattab (may Allah be pleased with him): A Beacon of Leadership for All Time

Omar ibn al-Khattab (may Allah be pleased with him) is one of the most honored and revered figures in Islamic history, embodying the very essence of justice, humility, and visionary leadership as prescribed by Islam. Born in Mecca around 584 CE, he was a member of the esteemed Quraysh tribe. Although Omar initially opposed the message of Islam, his heart was transformed, and after his conversion in 616 CE, he became one of the closest and most trusted companions of the Prophet Muhammad (peace be upon him). His conversion marked the beginning of an illustrious journey, during which he played a pivotal role in defending and advancing the cause of Islam.

After the passing of the Prophet Muhammad (peace be upon him), Omar (may Allah be pleased with him) took on an instrumental role in the development of the nascent Islamic state. After the caliphate of Abu Bakr (may Allah be pleased with him), Omar was appointed as the second caliph in 634 CE. During his caliphate, he guided the Muslim Ummah through a period of remarkable expansion and reform, marked by his profound sense of justice and equity. His leadership was instrumental in the rapid growth of the Islamic empire, as vast territories across the Byzantine and Sassanian empires came under Islamic rule. Yet, his true greatness lay not merely in conquest but in his ability to govern with wisdom, justice, and mercy.

The caliphate of Omar ibn al-Khattab (may Allah be pleased with him) is often referred to as a golden era of Islamic governance. His commitment to justice, treating both Muslims and non-Muslims with fairness and compassion, set an unparalleled standard for leadership that transcended divisions of faith, ethnicity, and status. Under his rule, systems of administration, governance, and law were established to ensure the welfare of all citizens. He was known for his personal humility, leading by example, living simply, and refusing special privileges, even as he held one of the most powerful positions in the world. Omar's emphasis on accountability, both for himself and his governors, fostered a culture of transparency and integrity, a model for leadership that remains timeless.

In today's world, where political corruption, inequality, and struggles for power often prevail, the example set by Omar ibn al-Khattab (may Allah be pleased with him) serves as a shining reminder of what true leadership entails. His leadership was not solely about expanding the empire or asserting control; it was deeply rooted in the principles of justice, fairness, and service to the people—values that resonate with the teachings of Islam. His leadership serves as an invaluable lesson for today's leaders, emphasizing that power coupled with humility, justice, and compassion can transform societies and create legacies that endure for generations.

The relevance of Omar's leadership is perhaps even more striking today. As the world faces increasingly complex challenges, ethical leadership rooted in justice, transparency, and compassion has become a rare yet essential need. In a time where trust in political and corporate leaders is waning, Omar's life offers a model for governing with integrity and empathy, ensuring the welfare of all people regardless of their status or faith. His ability to balance strength with compassion, his insistence on justice, and his unwavering commitment to the welfare of all under his rule illustrate how true leadership can unite and uplift a diverse and expansive community.

This book delves into the core principles that defined Omar ibn al-Khattab's leadership, presenting them as vital lessons for modern leaders and politicians. Through an in-depth exploration of his life, his decisions, and his legacy, we will uncover the traits that made him a truly exemplary leader: his profound sense of justice, his humility in wielding power, his respect for diversity, and his unwavering commitment to accountability. The chapters that follow will explore how these timeless principles shaped his rule and how they can be applied to today's leadership challenges in politics, business, and governance.

The leadership of Omar ibn al-Khattab (may Allah be pleased with him) is not merely a relic of history. It is a beacon of light that continues to illuminate the path for those seeking to lead with purpose, integrity, and compassion. The principles of justice, accountability, and mercy that he so fully embodied remain as relevant today as they were during his time. By learning from his legacy, leaders today can work toward building more just, fair, and compassionate societies.

As we journey through the life and lessons of Omar ibn al-Khattab (may Allah be pleased with him), it becomes clear that his leadership offers invaluable guidance for those who seek to lead with justice, fairness, and empathy. His legacy is one that endures far beyond his tenure as caliph, providing timeless principles for leadership that continue to inspire and uplift those in positions of authority today.

Omar ibn al-Khattab (may Allah be pleased with him): A Pillar of Justice in Early Islamic History

OMAR IBN AL-KHATTAB (may Allah be pleased with him) is one of the most esteemed and influential figures in Islamic history. Born into the powerful Quraysh tribe of Mecca in 584 CE, Omar initially stood as a strong opponent of Islam, resisting the message of the

Prophet Muhammad (peace be upon him). However, in a remarkable turn of events, Omar embraced Islam during the seventh year of the Prophet's mission. His conversion marked a pivotal moment for the Muslim community, as Omar's strength, wisdom, and leadership skills would soon become critical to the defense and expansion of the Islamic faith.

Omar's significance in Islamic history extends far beyond his early support for the Prophet Muhammad (peace be upon him). After the Prophet's passing, the Muslim Ummah faced the challenge of establishing stable governance. Omar played an instrumental role in securing the leadership of Abu Bakr (may Allah be pleased with him) as the first caliph. After Abu Bakr's passing, Omar was chosen as his successor, becoming the second caliph of the Rashidun Caliphate in 634 CE. For the next decade, until his martyrdom in 644 CE, Omar led the Muslim empire with unparalleled dedication and justice.

During his caliphate, Omar oversaw a period of tremendous territorial expansion, capturing regions that now comprise parts of modern-day Iraq, Syria, Palestine, Egypt, and Persia. These conquests, however, were not driven by a desire for power or wealth; they were grounded in a deep sense of responsibility to spread Islam's moral and ethical values, and to ensure justice and order. Omar's leadership was characterized by his relentless commitment to the rights of all people, whether Muslim or non-Muslim, ensuring that the conquered peoples were treated with fairness and that their religious and civil rights were preserved.

What distinguishes Omar as a leader was his profound sense of justice and his compassionate governance. His goal was not merely to expand the empire but to create a society built on fairness, equality, and the well-being of all its inhabitants. Omar instituted the first welfare programs in Islamic history, ensuring that the poor, orphans, and widows were supported. His legal reforms laid the foundation for Islamic jurisprudence, and he appointed judges throughout the empire to oversee the fair application of the law. His insistence on equality before the law—regardless of wealth, status, or power—earned him the lasting title of a just ruler.

In addition to his political and military leadership, Omar was known for his deep faith and personal humility. Despite ruling a vast and powerful empire, he lived a simple life, wearing modest clothing and often going without food so that others could eat. He would walk the streets at night to ensure that his people were being treated fairly and that their needs were met. His famous statement, "If a mule were to stumble on the banks of the Euphrates, I would fear that Allah would hold me accountable for not having leveled the road for it," demonstrates his profound sense of responsibility toward even the most vulnerable creatures under his rule.

Omar's leadership style has become a benchmark for Islamic governance. His reign not only saw the Islamic empire grow in size, but it also laid the groundwork for a just, equitable society that earned the respect of both Muslims and non-Muslims alike. His governance was not about dominance, but about ensuring justice, fairness, and compassion for all.

Omar ibn al-Khattab's legacy is defined not only by his territorial conquests or administrative reforms but also by the ethical framework he established for governance. His principles of justice, fairness, and accountability remain as relevant today as they were during his time. The way he ruled—with firmness, compassion, and a deep sense of responsibility to Allah and to his people—continues to be a model of leadership for all who seek to govern with integrity.

Omar's caliphate represents a crucial chapter in Islamic history. Under his leadership, the foundations of governance, law, and social welfare were firmly established in accordance with Islamic principles. His impact on the Islamic world and his model of leadership remain relevant today, offering timeless lessons for those in positions of authority who aspire to lead with justice, fairness, and a deep sense of duty to the people they serve.

The Enduring Relevance of Omar's Leadership in Modern Times

OMAR IBN AL-KHATTAB (may Allah be pleased with him) remains one of the most exemplary leaders in history, offering timeless lessons that are incredibly relevant to today's modern political and leadership challenges. In a world often marked by power struggles, corruption, inequality, and a disconnect between leaders and the people they serve, Omar's approach to governance stands as a beacon of ethical leadership. His ability to wield immense power while staying grounded in humility, justice, and accountability makes his life a source of inspiration for leaders across all sectors.

One of the key reasons why Omar's leadership principles are so vital today is his deep commitment to **justice and fairness**. In an era where many leaders face accusations of favoritism, corruption, and inequality, Omar's example shows how power can be exercised with integrity and equity. He did not just rule for the benefit of the elite or a specific group; rather, he saw it as his divine duty to ensure that every person under his rule—whether Muslim or non-Muslim—received fair treatment. Modern leaders, whether in politics, business, or any other domain, can benefit from studying how Omar upheld justice, often going to great lengths to ensure that no one was wronged under his governance.

Furthermore, Omar's **humility in power** offers a crucial lesson for today's leaders. In a world where many in positions of authority indulge in personal privilege and seek to elevate themselves above others, Omar's simplicity and modesty remain deeply relevant. He famously refused to adopt the luxuries of power, living simply and remaining close to the people. His life illustrates how humility in leadership fosters trust and respect, traits that are often lacking in modern politics. Leaders today, who sometimes seem distant or out of touch with their constituents, can learn from Omar's commitment to staying connected with the people and ensuring their welfare.

Another reason Omar's leadership matters in the modern world is his **respect for diversity and inclusiveness**. In an increasingly globalized world, where societies are becoming more diverse, leaders are challenged to create unity while respecting the differences among their people. Omar set an extraordinary example in this regard. His governance of non-Muslim communities, especially during the conquest of Jerusalem, demonstrated tolerance and protection for religious minorities. He showed how a leader could ensure the security and well-being of all citizens, regardless of their faith or background. Today, with rising tensions around issues of race, religion, and identity, leaders can greatly benefit from Omar's example of inclusiveness, ensuring that all people feel valued and protected under their leadership.

Omar's leadership was also characterized by his **accountability**. He believed that those in power should not only hold others accountable but also answer for their own actions. He famously walked the streets at night, disguised, to hear firsthand the concerns and struggles of his people, ensuring that his governors and officials were serving them justly. In contrast, modern leaders often face criticism for a lack of transparency and accountability, with many placing themselves above scrutiny. Omar's life serves as a reminder that true leadership is about serving the people and being answerable to them, a principle that could restore public trust in leadership today.

In addition to these qualities, Omar's **long-term vision and strategic thinking** made his leadership effective and sustainable. His administrative reforms, welfare programs, and military strategies were not short-term fixes but were designed to benefit future generations. In the fast-paced modern world, where leaders are often focused on immediate results, Omar's ability to think beyond the present moment is an invaluable lesson. His vision for the Islamic empire was not just about expansion; it was about building a just society that would last. Leaders today can learn from this approach by focusing on policies and decisions that bring lasting benefits rather than seeking short-term gains or political victories.

Omar also exemplified the value of **empathy and compassion** in leadership. His concern for the poor, widows, and orphans, and his establishment of welfare systems, demonstrate the importance of prioritizing the vulnerable in society. In today's world, where economic disparity and social injustice remain widespread, Omar's emphasis on social welfare and caring for the underprivileged is a model for modern governance. Leaders who are mindful of the needs of the less fortunate, as Omar was, are more likely to create societies that are both prosperous and just.

Ultimately, Omar's leadership matters today because it is a powerful reminder of what leadership is truly about: serving the people, acting with justice and fairness, and ruling with humility and accountability. In a world that often seems to prioritize power for its own sake, Omar's life and caliphate demonstrate that power should be used to uplift others, not for personal gain. His approach to leadership, deeply rooted in the principles of Islam, provides a framework for ethical and just governance that transcends time and place.

For modern leaders and politicians, studying Omar's leadership is not only an exercise in understanding history but also a practical guide for how to lead effectively and ethically. His unwavering commitment to justice, accountability, inclusiveness, and humility offers timeless lessons that can help restore trust in leadership and create more just and compassionate societies.

A Roadmap to Ethical Leadership: Key Lessons from Omar ibn al-Khattab

THIS BOOK AIMS TO DISTILL the timeless leadership principles of Omar ibn al-Khattab (may Allah be pleased with him) into actionable lessons for modern leaders and politicians. As we navigate the complexities of today's world—marked by political polarization, economic inequality, social unrest, and widespread distrust in leadership—Omar's life and governance offer a guiding light. His principles of justice, humility, accountability, and inclusiveness are not only relevant but urgently needed in today's leadership landscape.

At the heart of the book is Omar's unwavering commitment to **justice and fairness**. Throughout his caliphate, Omar ensured that all people, regardless of their background or faith, were treated justly under the law. This emphasis on fairness was a cornerstone of his governance and is a vital lesson for contemporary leaders. In a world where inequality is rising and many feel left behind by their leaders, embracing justice as a foundational principle can help restore trust in governance and create more equitable societies.

The book also delves deeply into the concept of **humility in power**. Omar, despite his immense authority, led a simple life, demonstrating that true leadership does not require extravagance or privilege. His humility earned him the respect and admiration of those he led. This lesson is particularly relevant in today's political and business environments, where many leaders seem distant from the people they serve. Humility in leadership fosters connection and trust, making it easier for leaders to engage with and understand the needs of their constituents.

Another key lesson explored in the book is **respect for diversity and inclusiveness**. Omar's protection of religious minorities and his policies of tolerance, particularly during the conquest of Jerusalem, serve as a model for modern leadership in our increasingly multicultural and globalized world. Leaders today must manage diversity with care, ensuring that all groups—regardless of race, religion, or background—are valued and their rights protected. Omar's example provides a powerful lesson on how to create unity and stability by embracing inclusiveness and protecting the rights of all.

Accountability is another cornerstone of Omar's leadership that the book highlights. Unlike many modern leaders who distance themselves from responsibility, Omar held himself accountable to the people. He actively sought out their concerns and made sure that his governors were serving justly. This sense of accountability is essential for restoring public confidence in leadership. By holding themselves to high standards and being transparent in their actions, today's leaders can inspire trust and foster loyalty among the people they serve.

The book also emphasizes Omar's **long-term vision.** His administrative and social reforms were designed not just for immediate gains but for the long-term prosperity of the Islamic empire. In today's fast-paced world, leaders are often pressured to focus on short-term results. Omar's leadership demonstrates the value of foresight and planning for future generations. By thinking beyond the immediate, modern leaders can build sustainable systems that ensure long-term growth and stability.

Another vital lesson is Omar's **empathy and compassion.** His concern for the poor, the widows, and the orphans led to the establishment of social welfare programs, ensuring that the most vulnerable were cared for. This emphasis on social welfare is a crucial lesson for today's leaders, who must address the needs of marginalized groups and ensure that no one is left behind. Compassionate leadership, as modeled by Omar, helps to create a more just and balanced society.

In essence, the book provides a comprehensive examination of how Omar's leadership principles can be applied to the modern world. It takes each core principle—justice, humility, accountability, inclusiveness, vision, and empathy—and shows how these timeless values can address the challenges faced by contemporary leaders. Whether one is navigating the political arena, leading a business, or guiding a community, Omar's leadership style offers enduring lessons that can help create a more just, fair, and compassionate society.

Through this book, readers will gain insights into how they can lead with integrity and purpose, following in the footsteps of one of history's greatest leaders. By applying the lessons from Omar's life and caliphate, modern leaders have the opportunity to create lasting positive change, build trust with their people, and ensure that their leadership serves not just the powerful, but all members of society.

Part I: Foundations of Ethical Leadership: Justice, Humility, and Inclusiveness

The foundations of effective and ethical leadership can often be traced back to core principles that transcend time, culture, and circumstance. In the case of Omar ibn al-Khattab (may Allah be pleased with him), these foundational principles—justice, humility, and respect for diversity—formed the bedrock of his governance and continue to offer vital lessons for modern leaders. His leadership was not merely about wielding power or expanding territories; it was about ensuring that those under his rule, regardless of their faith or status, were treated with fairness, dignity, and compassion.

One of the defining aspects of Omar's leadership was his deep commitment to **justice and fairness**. His approach to governance revolved around ensuring that every individual, from the most powerful to the most vulnerable, received equal treatment under the law. This was not a theoretical ideal; it was a practical, lived reality during his caliphate. He held himself accountable even for the welfare of animals in his domain, famously declaring that if a mule were to stumble on the banks of the Euphrates River, he would feel responsible before Allah for not having made the road smooth. This profound sense of accountability and fairness set the tone for his entire rule. Justice, for Omar, was not simply a function of maintaining order but an essential element in building trust between the ruler and the ruled. His sense of fairness extended to non-Muslims under his rule, ensuring that they were protected and allowed to practice their faith freely. For modern leaders, this offers a critical lesson: justice is the cornerstone of stability and trust in governance. When people feel that they are treated fairly, they are more likely to support their leaders and work toward a common good.

Equally important to Omar's legacy is his **humility in power**. Despite being one of the most powerful figures of his time, Omar led a life of remarkable modesty. He refused to indulge in the privileges of his position, opting instead to live in simplicity, which allowed him to stay close to the people he served. This was most clearly illustrated during his famous entry into Jerusalem, where he arrived in humble clothing, walking beside his servant, and taking turns riding a camel. His humility was not a show; it was a reflection of his deep belief that leadership was a responsibility rather than a privilege. Modern leaders, particularly in positions of significant power, often struggle with staying grounded. Omar's example teaches that true greatness is found in remaining humble and connected to the needs of the people, regardless of one's status. Cultivating humility allows leaders to avoid the trappings of arrogance, which can lead to detachment from those they govern.

Omar's leadership was also marked by his **respect for diversity and inclusiveness**. At a time when religious and cultural differences often led to division and conflict, Omar's treatment of non-Muslims under his rule stands out as a model of tolerance and respect. One of the most notable examples of this was his protection of Christian sites during the conquest of Jerusalem. Instead of desecrating or converting these places of worship, he ensured their preservation and allowed Christians to continue practicing their faith without fear. This respect for religious diversity was not just a political tactic; it was rooted in his understanding of justice and fairness. In today's world, where leaders are faced with increasingly diverse populations, Omar's example highlights the importance of inclusiveness. Tolerance, empathy, and the protection of minority rights are not just moral imperatives but are crucial for creating harmony and unity in society.

By grounding his leadership in justice, humility, and respect for diversity, Omar ibn al-Khattab demonstrated that effective governance is not about exercising control but about serving the people with fairness and compassion. These foundational principles are just as relevant today as they were during Omar's time. Leaders who prioritize justice build trust; those who lead with humility inspire loyalty; and those who respect diversity foster peace and unity. In the chapters that follow, each of these principles will be explored in greater detail, offering lessons that can be directly applied to the challenges of modern leadership. Through the lens of Omar's leadership, we can see how the values of the past can guide the leaders of today toward building more just, inclusive, and effective societies.

Chapter 1: Justice and Fairness: The Cornerstone of Omar's Leadership

The principle of justice was at the very heart of Omar ibn al-Khattab's (may Allah be pleased with him) leadership. Throughout his caliphate, his commitment to ensuring fairness for all—regardless of faith, status, or wealth—defined the way he governed the growing Islamic empire. Justice for Omar was not an abstract concept; it was the driving force behind every decision he made. His belief in the importance of fairness extended from the wealthiest members of society down to the most vulnerable creatures, as illustrated by one of his famous statements: "If a mule were to stumble on the banks of the Euphrates, I would fear that Allah would hold me accountable for not having leveled the road for it."

This deep sense of personal responsibility characterized Omar's approach to leadership and is reflected in numerous stories from his time as caliph. One such story tells of a time when a man came to Omar to complain about an unjust governor. Rather than dismiss the man's concerns or defend his appointed official, Omar investigated the matter personally. When he found that the governor had indeed acted unjustly, he immediately removed him from power, emphasizing that no one—regardless of their position—was above the law. This insistence on accountability created a culture of transparency within his administration, where both leaders and citizens knew that justice would always prevail.

Omar also took measures to ensure that justice extended beyond the Muslim community. His treatment of non-Muslims living under

Islamic rule exemplified his commitment to fairness. When Jerusalem was peacefully conquered, he made it a point to guarantee the safety of the Christian and Jewish communities, allowing them to practice their faith freely and protecting their places of worship. By ensuring that all citizens, regardless of their religion, were treated equally, Omar built a society where trust and cooperation flourished. This inclusiveness, rooted in justice, enabled the empire to grow without alienating those who were under its protection.

For modern leaders, the lesson is clear: justice and fairness are the foundation upon which trust in leadership is built. When people see that their leaders are fair, they are more likely to trust their decisions and cooperate for the greater good. In times of crisis or conflict, a leader who consistently upholds justice will find it easier to rally support and maintain stability. Fairness fosters loyalty because people feel secure in the knowledge that they will be treated equitably, no matter their circumstances.

The practical application of justice in leadership can take many forms today. One of the first steps modern leaders can take is to establish transparent systems of accountability, ensuring that no one in their administration is above the law. By holding themselves and others accountable for their actions, leaders demonstrate that fairness is a guiding principle, not a convenience. Furthermore, ensuring that policies and decisions are made with equity in mind—whether in the workplace, in government, or in any leadership capacity—can promote a sense of justice within the community.

Another way leaders can prioritize fairness is by listening to the grievances of their people, just as Omar did. When individuals feel unheard, it can breed resentment and instability. A leader who is accessible, open to hearing the concerns of all, and willing to act on those concerns strengthens the bond between themselves and those they lead. Justice does not always require grand actions; it often begins with small, everyday acts of fairness that reflect a leader's commitment to the welfare of all.

Omar's approach to justice is a timeless model that shows the power of fairness in governance. It is not simply a means to maintain order but a moral duty that leaders owe to those they serve. Justice builds trust, and with trust comes the stability and cooperation necessary for a society to thrive. Modern leaders who adopt Omar's approach will find that by upholding fairness, they are laying the foundation for lasting and effective leadership.

Omar's Unwavering Commitment to Justice

OMAR IBN AL-KHATTAB (may Allah be pleased with him) is renowned for his deep and unwavering commitment to justice, a value that guided his every decision during his time as the caliph. His leadership was marked by an acute awareness that he would be held accountable by Allah for how he governed, and this sense of responsibility extended to every aspect of his rule. Justice, for Omar, was not just about maintaining social order or enforcing laws; it was about ensuring that every person—regardless of their religion, status, or background—was treated fairly and equitably. His approach to justice has left a lasting legacy in Islamic history, inspiring leaders for generations.

One of the most famous examples of Omar's sense of justice comes from a statement he made about the well-being of even the animals under his rule. He famously declared, "If a mule were to stumble on the banks of the Euphrates, I would fear that Allah would hold me accountable for not having leveled the road for it." This powerful declaration illustrates Omar's profound sense of responsibility, not only for the people he governed but for every creature under his care. It was a reflection of his belief that justice required him to be mindful of the smallest details, ensuring that every living being in his empire was treated with care and fairness.

Beyond his concern for animals, Omar's approach to justice was most clearly demonstrated in how he dealt with his governors and officials. He was known for personally overseeing the actions of his appointees and holding them accountable when they acted unjustly. In one instance, a man came to Omar to complain about a governor who had wronged him. Rather than dismissing the man or ignoring his concerns, Omar took the complaint seriously and conducted a thorough investigation. When he found that the governor had indeed acted unjustly, he immediately removed the official from his position. This act sent a clear message: no one, not even the highest-ranking officials, was above the law. By holding those in power accountable, Omar ensured that justice remained a guiding principle throughout his administration.

Omar's sense of justice extended beyond the Muslim community as well. His treatment of non-Muslims, particularly during the conquest of Jerusalem, serves as another powerful example of his fairness. After the city's peaceful surrender, Omar personally ensured the safety and protection of Christian and Jewish communities. He met with the Christian Patriarch Sophronius and promised that their places of worship would not be harmed and that their religious practices would be respected. True to his word, Omar allowed Christians and Jews to live and worship freely under Islamic rule, setting an example of tolerance and justice that was rare for the time. His actions demonstrated that justice was not limited to Muslims; it was a universal principle that applied to all people under his governance.

Omar's reputation for justice also earned him the trust and loyalty of the people. His accessibility as a leader was unmatched, and he would often walk the streets at night, disguised, to hear firsthand the concerns of his citizens. This practice allowed him to stay connected with the people and ensured that their voices were heard. One famous story recounts how Omar, while patrolling the streets, overheard a woman expressing her frustration over the scarcity of food. Moved by her plight, Omar immediately took action, delivering food to her himself. This was a clear illustration of his belief that a just leader must be present and actively involved in the welfare of his people.

Through these stories and countless others, Omar's approach to justice can be seen as both practical and deeply moral. He understood that justice was the key to maintaining stability, trust, and peace within the community. His fairness was not simply a tool for governance but a reflection of his dedication to Allah and his responsibility as a caliph. Omar's sense of justice ensured that his leadership was not based on power or control but on serving the people with integrity and fairness.

Omar ibn al-Khattab's commitment to justice remains a timeless example of ethical leadership. His ability to balance strength with compassion, and his insistence that all people, regardless of their status, be treated with fairness, has left an enduring legacy in the annals of Islamic history. His approach to justice continues to offer valuable lessons for leaders today, demonstrating that true power lies in upholding justice for all.

The Power of Justice and Fairness in Modern Leadership

JUSTICE AND FAIRNESS are foundational pillars in leadership that build trust, foster stability, and cultivate loyalty among the people. Omar ibn al-Khattab's (may Allah be pleased with him) leadership demonstrates how the consistent application of these values can create a harmonious society and establish a legacy of respect and integrity. For modern leaders, the lesson is clear: justice is not only a moral imperative but a practical tool for creating a stable and cohesive environment, whether in governance, business, or any form of leadership.

When leaders commit to fairness, they set the tone for how their society or organization will function. Justice ensures that everyone is treated equally under the law or within the organization's rules, creating a sense of security and trust. People are more likely to trust leaders who are consistent and equitable in their decisions, knowing that they will not be subjected to favoritism, corruption, or unfair treatment. This trust, once established, forms the backbone of a stable and flourishing system where individuals feel safe, valued, and protected.

Omar's leadership is a prime example of how justice builds trust. His transparent and fair governance ensured that people, whether Muslim or non-Muslim, felt confident in his ability to rule justly. His insistence that even the most powerful were not above the law demonstrated that fairness was non-negotiable. Modern leaders can draw from this principle by ensuring that their policies and decisions are applied uniformly to all, without bias or favoritism. In the political realm, this might mean upholding the rule of law even when it is inconvenient for those in power. In business, it could involve maintaining consistent standards for employees and customers alike, regardless of their rank or influence.

Fairness in leadership also fosters **stability**. When people trust that their leaders are acting in their best interests and that justice will be upheld, they are more likely to support those leaders, even during difficult times. Conversely, when leaders are seen as unjust or corrupt, instability follows as people lose confidence in the system. Omar's governance was marked by stability, even as the Islamic empire expanded rapidly under his rule. This stability was a direct result of his fairness, as people across diverse cultures and backgrounds knew they would be treated justly under his leadership. Today, leaders who prioritize fairness can avoid unrest, discord, and the erosion of public trust, creating a stable environment where progress and cooperation are possible.

Justice is also an essential factor in **building loyalty**. People want to follow leaders they respect, and respect is earned through fairness.

Omar's accessibility, his commitment to listening to the grievances of the people, and his willingness to correct injustices—whether caused by his own governors or by systemic issues—fostered deep loyalty among his followers. In modern leadership, this principle remains relevant. Leaders who demonstrate that they are willing to stand up for justice, even when it's difficult, earn the respect and loyalty of those they lead. This loyalty is crucial in building teams, communities, or nations that work together toward shared goals.

Practically, modern leaders can implement justice and fairness in several ways. First, **transparency** is key. When leaders make their decision-making processes clear, they prevent accusations of bias or corruption. Open communication about how and why decisions are made can help build trust and ensure that people feel included in the process. Leaders can also institute **accountability measures** to ensure that everyone, including those in power, is held to the same standards. Omar's readiness to remove corrupt or unjust governors is a model for modern leadership, where accountability often becomes lax the higher one climbs in authority. Instituting regular checks and balances ensures that fairness remains at the heart of leadership.

Another practical way to ensure fairness is through **listening and empathy**. Leaders must make themselves available to hear the concerns of the people they serve. Omar's nighttime walks through Medina, where he disguised himself to hear the true state of his people's lives, show that leaders must go beyond formal channels to stay connected with those they lead. Today, leaders can implement feedback mechanisms, engage with people directly, and maintain a hands-on approach to governance or management. Being present and attentive to the needs and concerns of the people helps leaders stay grounded and act with justice.

In conclusion, justice and fairness are not abstract ideals but critical components of effective leadership. They build trust, create stability, and foster loyalty—all essential elements for long-term success. Omar ibn al-Khattab's example shows that when leaders prioritize fairness, they cultivate an environment where people feel valued, protected, and motivated to contribute positively to society. Modern leaders can apply these timeless lessons by remaining transparent, holding themselves accountable, and staying connected to the people they serve. By doing so, they lay the groundwork for a leadership legacy built on trust, respect, and justice for all.

Implementing Fairness and Justice in Modern Leadership

IN TODAY'S FAST-PACED world, leaders face the challenge of making decisions that affect diverse groups of people. To build trust, stability, and long-term success, it is essential that fairness and justice are at the core of every decision a leader makes. By learning from the example of Omar ibn al-Khattab (may Allah be pleased with him), modern leaders can prioritize these values in practical ways, ensuring that their leadership is both effective and ethical.

One of the first steps leaders can take to prioritize fairness is **establishing transparent decision-making processes**. Transparency is key to preventing misunderstandings, favoritism, and corruption. When leaders openly communicate the criteria behind their decisions—whether it's policy creation, hiring, promotions, or legal rulings—they allow others to see that fairness is being upheld. For example, in a business setting, leaders should outline clear guidelines for promotions and bonuses, ensuring that all employees understand how performance is evaluated. In governance, transparency about how resources are allocated or laws are enforced prevents feelings of exclusion or injustice.

Leaders must also **institutionalize accountability**, making it clear that no one is above the rules, including themselves. Omar's leadership exemplified this principle through his practice of holding governors and other officials accountable for their actions. In the modern world, leaders can achieve this by creating systems of checks and balances that apply to everyone. For example, in government, leaders can support the establishment of independent oversight bodies that monitor the actions of officials and ensure that laws are applied equally to all. In corporate settings, leaders can implement whistleblower policies and ethical review boards that hold employees and executives accountable for their actions, thus maintaining fairness throughout the organization.

Listening to the concerns of the people is another vital way to ensure justice in leadership. Omar regularly sought out the opinions and grievances of his people, often going to great lengths to understand their struggles firsthand. Modern leaders, too, can implement effective feedback mechanisms that allow individuals at all levels to express their concerns without fear of retribution. This could be done through regular town hall meetings, surveys, open-door policies, or digital platforms where people can submit feedback anonymously. Leaders who actively listen demonstrate that they value the voices of those they lead and are willing to make adjustments based on the feedback they receive.

Empathy plays a crucial role in promoting fairness. Leaders need to put themselves in the shoes of those affected by their decisions. Omar's concern for the poor, orphans, and widows—ensuring that their rights were protected and their needs met—can inspire modern leaders to prioritize **social welfare and inclusivity** in their decision-making. In practice, this could mean ensuring that policies or programs do not disproportionately affect vulnerable groups. For example, when developing healthcare policies, leaders should consider how changes might impact low-income families and work to make solutions accessible for everyone. In business, leaders can introduce fair wage practices, ensuring that employees at all levels receive compensation that reflects their contribution and sustains their livelihood.

Another practical application of fairness is **ensuring equal access to opportunities**. Whether in a government or corporate setting, leaders should create environments where merit and effort are the primary criteria for advancement, rather than personal connections, background, or favoritism. Leaders can establish mentorship programs, provide education and training opportunities for all employees, and create pathways for advancement that are open and accessible to everyone. For example, offering professional development courses for underrepresented groups can level the playing field and foster an inclusive environment where everyone has the chance to succeed based on their merit.

Being present and engaged is another way leaders can ensure that justice remains a priority. Omar's famous nighttime walks among the people allowed him to see firsthand how his decisions affected their lives, which informed his future actions. Modern leaders can take a similar approach by staying engaged with their teams or communities. This can involve visiting worksites, holding open discussions with employees or constituents, and directly observing the effects of their policies. By engaging with the people they serve, leaders can better understand the real-world impact of their decisions and adjust accordingly to promote fairness.

Lastly, leaders can promote fairness by **creating diverse teams** that reflect the broader community or organization. When leadership is diverse, it becomes more likely that a wide range of perspectives will be considered, leading to more equitable decisions. For instance, in a company, a diverse leadership team can offer varied insights into how different groups of employees or customers might be affected by a decision. This helps prevent bias and ensures that decisions are fair and just for everyone involved.

In conclusion, fairness and justice are not abstract ideals but essential components of strong and effective leadership. Modern leaders can prioritize these values through transparency, accountability, active listening, empathy, and inclusiveness. By taking practical steps to ensure fairness in their decision-making processes, leaders can build trust, promote stability, and foster a more just and equitable environment for all. Omar ibn al-Khattab's leadership provides a timeless example of how prioritizing justice not only creates harmony but also establishes a lasting legacy of integrity and respect.

Chapter 2: Humility in Power: The Quiet Strength of Omar ibn al-Khattab

True power does not need to be announced through grand gestures or extravagant displays. Omar ibn al-Khattab (may Allah be pleased with him) understood this deeply. Throughout his leadership, he demonstrated that humility is one of the greatest strengths a leader can possess. Despite ruling an expansive and rapidly growing empire, Omar lived modestly, never allowing the trappings of power to cloud his judgment or disconnect him from the people. His leadership showed that remaining humble and grounded, even when wielding immense authority, is essential for maintaining trust and respect.

Omar's modesty is perhaps best captured in his famous entry into Jerusalem after the peaceful conquest of the city. Unlike many rulers of his time, who would have used such a moment to showcase their power and wealth, Omar arrived in Jerusalem in the simplest of manners. He wore modest clothes and shared a camel with his servant, taking turns riding it as they approached the city. When it was the servant's turn to ride, Omar walked, leading the camel, without concern for how this might appear to others. This act was not a performance but a reflection of his deep belief that leadership was about service, not personal glorification.

This humility extended to every aspect of Omar's life. He lived in a modest home, often ate simple meals, and resisted the temptation to accumulate wealth or luxuries. Despite being the caliph, one of the most powerful figures of his time, he chose to live like an ordinary man, closer to the people he served. His modest lifestyle and humility made him relatable, accessible, and deeply respected by his followers. Omar's humility allowed him to lead with integrity, free from the distractions of excess or pride. It also ensured that he remained focused on the well-being of his people, rather than being consumed by the privileges of his position.

For modern leaders, Omar's example offers a powerful lesson: staying grounded and humble, especially when in positions of authority, fosters stronger connections with those being led. In today's world, where leaders are often elevated to almost unreachable heights, humility is more important than ever. Leaders who remain humble show that they are in touch with the reality of the people's lives and are willing to listen, learn, and grow. This creates an environment of trust, where people feel valued and respected, rather than distanced from those in power.

The cultivation of humility in leadership begins with a mindset shift. Leaders must recognize that their position is a responsibility, not a privilege. Omar viewed his role as a duty to Allah and the people, not as an opportunity for self-advancement. Modern leaders can emulate this by seeing their positions as opportunities to serve, rather than to amass personal gain. This shift in perspective helps leaders avoid arrogance, ensuring that their decisions are always made with the welfare of others in mind.

Another practical way for leaders to cultivate humility is through **engagement with the people**. Omar's accessibility, his walks through the streets of Medina, and his personal involvement in resolving the people's concerns, kept him connected to the reality of those he governed. Modern leaders can achieve this by maintaining open lines of communication, being present in their communities or organizations, and actively seeking feedback. Whether it's holding regular meetings with employees, making time for one-on-one interactions, or directly observing the effects of their policies, leaders who stay engaged demonstrate that they are not above the people they lead.

Leaders can also practice humility by **sharing credit and acknowledging mistakes**. Omar was never one to claim sole credit for successes or achievements; he often recognized the contributions of others and admitted when he needed guidance or counsel. In today's leadership environment, where taking personal credit and avoiding blame can be common, leaders can stand out by celebrating the efforts of their teams and acknowledging their own shortcomings. This not only fosters a culture of trust and collaboration but also sets a powerful example for others.

Leading by example is perhaps the most powerful way to cultivate humility. Omar's actions—whether it was walking beside his servant into Jerusalem or living a simple life while ruling a vast empire—were a reflection of his values. Modern leaders can embody humility by leading with integrity and consistently modeling the behavior they expect from others. This could mean engaging in the day-to-day work of the team, showing empathy in decision-making, or foregoing unnecessary luxuries to stay connected to the core mission. When leaders live humbly, they set a tone that permeates the organization or community, creating an environment of mutual respect and shared purpose.

In conclusion, Omar ibn al-Khattab's life shows that humility is not a weakness but a quiet strength that enhances leadership. His modesty and simplicity, even in the face of immense power, earned him the respect and loyalty of his people. In today's world, where leaders are often disconnected from those they serve, humility is more important than ever. By staying grounded, engaging with others, sharing credit, and leading by example, modern leaders can cultivate humility, ensuring that their leadership is marked by integrity, respect, and trust.

Omar's Modesty and Simplicity: Leadership

Through Humility

OMAR IBN AL-KHATTAB (may Allah be pleased with him) is remembered not only for his strength and justice but also for his profound humility and modesty in the face of power. Despite ruling a vast empire and being one of the most influential leaders of his time, Omar chose a life of simplicity, reflecting his deep commitment to serving the people rather than elevating himself above them. His humble lifestyle was a testament to his belief that true leadership is not about material wealth or outward displays of power but about responsibility, service, and staying grounded in the principles of justice and fairness.

One of the most famous and symbolic examples of Omar's humility is his entry into Jerusalem after its peaceful conquest in 637 CE. As the caliph of the rapidly expanding Islamic empire, Omar could have chosen to enter the city with pomp and ceremony, showcasing the might of his rule. Instead, he arrived in the simplest of manners. He wore modest clothes, a sign of his refusal to adopt the luxuries often associated with leadership. Even more striking, Omar shared a camel with his servant for the journey, taking turns riding it. As they approached the city, it was the servant's turn to ride, and Omar, without hesitation, walked beside the camel, holding its reins. This act astonished the people of Jerusalem, including the Christian Patriarch Sophronius, who expected the leader of such a powerful empire to arrive with grandeur. Omar's entry into Jerusalem is a profound example of his belief that leadership should be marked by humility, not by pride or excess.

Omar's modesty was not just a momentary act for display; it was a reflection of how he lived his life every day. He refused to indulge in the privileges that came with his position as caliph. While he had access to wealth and luxury, Omar chose to live simply, in a modest home, wearing simple clothes, and eating basic meals. He did not separate himself from the everyday lives of the people he led. He often went without food so that he could experience the hunger his people felt, making sure that he never distanced himself from their struggles. This personal choice to live humbly was a powerful message to the Muslim community, showing that even the caliph was subject to the same conditions as the people.

One story from Omar's caliphate highlights his humble nature. During a time of drought and famine, Omar took it upon himself to ensure that the people were fed, even while he personally abstained from eating anything luxurious. When food supplies became scarce, Omar imposed strict rationing on himself, eating nothing more than bread and olive oil, while his body weakened and grew visibly thin. When others around him tried to convince him to eat better for his own health, Omar refused, saying that he could not eat lavishly while those under his care went hungry. This act of self-denial showed his deep empathy for the people and his understanding that a leader must share in the burdens of those he governs.

Omar's humility also extended to his interactions with others. He was known for his accessibility and for living among the people rather than in isolated luxury. He would often walk the streets at night, disguised, to hear firsthand about the problems and concerns of the community. This practice allowed him to govern with a deep understanding of the lives of ordinary people, ensuring that his decisions were grounded in their realities. He did not consider himself above reproach and was open to criticism, demonstrating his belief that leadership was a responsibility, not a privilege.

In another famous incident, a man confronted Omar publicly, criticizing his actions. Instead of reacting with anger or defensiveness, Omar thanked the man for pointing out the issue and took immediate steps to rectify the situation. This openness to feedback and his willingness to admit mistakes was a hallmark of his humility. It showed that, despite his immense power, Omar remained deeply connected to the principles of justice, fairness, and service to the community.

Omar's humility was not only an example of personal virtue but also a leadership style that inspired respect and loyalty from the people. By living simply and maintaining his connection to the everyday struggles of those he led, he fostered a sense of trust and solidarity between himself and the community. His modesty allowed him to lead with integrity, ensuring that his decisions were always made with the welfare of the people in mind, rather than for personal gain or glory.

In a world where power is often accompanied by displays of wealth and status, Omar's humility stands as a powerful reminder that true leadership is grounded in modesty and service. His example teaches modern leaders that it is possible to hold great authority while remaining humble, accessible, and committed to the well-being of those they lead. Omar's life is a testament to the fact that the most respected and effective leaders are those who prioritize the needs of the people over personal privilege, and who lead not from a place of pride, but from a place of humility and compassion.

Staying Grounded: The Power of Humility in Leadership

ONE OF THE MOST CRUCIAL lessons modern leaders can draw from Omar ibn al-Khattab's (may Allah be pleased with him) leadership is the value of remaining grounded and humble, even when placed in positions of immense power. In today's world, where leadership roles often come with elevated status, wealth, and privilege, the ability to stay humble is not only a rare trait but also a powerful tool for effective leadership. Humility, far from being a sign of weakness, is a reflection of inner strength, maturity, and confidence. It enables leaders to connect with those they serve, earn their trust, and inspire genuine loyalty.

Omar's life provides a profound example of how humility can enhance leadership. Despite being the caliph of a vast empire, he lived simply, wore modest clothing, and refused to indulge in the luxuries that his position afforded him. This humility did not diminish his authority; rather, it enhanced his ability to lead because it allowed him to relate to the everyday struggles of the people. His humility also set a powerful example for those around him, reinforcing the idea that leadership is a form of service, not a platform for personal glorification.

For modern leaders, the importance of staying grounded in humility is paramount. In a world where leaders are often placed on pedestals, surrounded by wealth, and distanced from the realities of ordinary life, it is easy to lose touch with the people they are meant to serve. Humility helps prevent this disconnection, keeping leaders accessible and relatable. Leaders who remain grounded understand the challenges faced by their people because they do not isolate themselves from them. This connection fosters trust and respect, as people are more likely to follow someone who they believe genuinely understands and cares about their needs.

Moreover, humility allows leaders to make better decisions. When leaders are humble, they are more open to feedback and willing to listen to others, which leads to more informed and balanced decision-making. Leaders who cultivate humility understand that they do not have all the answers and are willing to seek counsel from those with different perspectives or more expertise in specific areas. This openness to learning and self-reflection makes them more effective and adaptive leaders. In contrast, arrogance or a sense of superiority can blind leaders to their own shortcomings and lead to poor decision-making.

Another critical aspect of humility is the ability to admit mistakes. No leader is perfect, and those who acknowledge their errors demonstrate both honesty and accountability—traits that inspire confidence in others. Omar was known for admitting his mistakes and thanking those who pointed out his flaws. This transparency in leadership not only fosters trust but also encourages a culture of honesty within the organization or community. Modern leaders who practice humility are not afraid of being vulnerable because they understand that admitting faults is a strength, not a weakness.

Humility also helps leaders avoid the corruption of power. When leaders become too comfortable with privilege or power, it can lead to a sense of entitlement and arrogance. They may begin to prioritize their interests over the well-being of those they lead, resulting in unethical behavior or abuses of power. Omar's humility acted as a safeguard against such corruption. By living simply and holding himself accountable to the same standards as everyone else, he avoided the temptations that often come with authority. For modern leaders, humility is a check on ego, ensuring that they remain focused on their responsibilities rather than succumbing to personal desires or ambitions.

Leaders who stay grounded in humility also foster stronger, more cohesive teams. Humble leaders recognize the contributions of others, share credit for successes, and are more likely to create an environment where everyone feels valued. This collaborative atmosphere encourages creativity, innovation, and loyalty. People are more motivated to work for a leader who acknowledges their efforts and makes them feel like part of a team, rather than for someone who takes all the credit and distances themselves from the group.

In today's rapidly changing and often divided world, humility is a vital trait that can bring people together and create a sense of unity. Leaders who are humble can bridge gaps between themselves and others, making it easier to resolve conflicts and find common ground. Humility fosters empathy, as it requires leaders to put themselves in the shoes of others and consider how their actions affect those around them. This ability to empathize with others' perspectives is essential for modern leaders who are tasked with leading diverse teams or communities with varying needs and interests.

Ultimately, humility helps leaders stay focused on their true purpose: serving the people. Omar's humility was rooted in his deep sense of responsibility to Allah and the people he led. He never saw his role as caliph as a personal achievement but as a trust that he needed to fulfill with integrity and fairness. For modern leaders, staying humble ensures that their leadership remains grounded in the values of service, justice, and compassion, rather than being driven by ego or ambition.

In conclusion, humility is one of the most powerful qualities a leader can possess. It keeps leaders connected to the people they serve, fosters better decision-making, encourages accountability, and protects against the corrupting influence of power. By following Omar's example and cultivating humility, modern leaders can build trust, inspire loyalty, and lead with integrity, ensuring that their leadership is both effective and ethical. Humility is not a sign of weakness but the foundation of true strength in leadership.

Cultivating Humility: Practical Steps for Modern Leaders

IN A WORLD WHERE LEADERSHIP is often associated with power, prestige, and authority, staying humble can be a challenge. Yet, humility remains one of the most important qualities that a leader can cultivate. It not only strengthens relationships with those being led but also guards against the pitfalls of arrogance and detachment. For modern leaders, humility is essential for building trust, fostering collaboration, and staying connected to the people they serve. By following practical steps, leaders can cultivate humility and avoid the ego traps that often accompany positions of power.

One of the most effective ways for leaders to cultivate humility is by **staying connected to the everyday experiences of the people they lead.** Just as Omar ibn al-Khattab (may Allah be pleased with him) walked the streets of Medina to hear firsthand the concerns of the people, modern leaders should strive to remain engaged with those they serve. This could involve regular, direct interactions with employees or constituents, conducting visits to different departments or communities, or simply creating open forums where people can share their experiences and concerns. By making time for these interactions, leaders show that they are willing to listen and learn, reinforcing the idea that leadership is about service, not status.

Acknowledging mistakes and taking responsibility is another critical practice for cultivating humility. No leader is infallible, and being willing to admit errors demonstrates both honesty and a willingness to learn. Leaders who admit their mistakes create a culture of openness, where team members feel comfortable taking risks and speaking up without fear of harsh repercussions. This fosters a more innovative and collaborative environment. In contrast, leaders who refuse to acknowledge their errors or shift blame onto others foster resentment and a lack of trust. By being transparent about their own shortcomings, leaders show that they are human and focused on growth, rather than protecting their ego.

Modern leaders can also cultivate humility by **sharing credit and recognizing the contributions of others**. Too often, leadership is associated with taking all the glory for successes while deflecting responsibility for failures. This approach can create resentment within teams or organizations, as people feel their hard work is being overlooked. Leaders who practice humility, however, make it a priority to celebrate the achievements of others and recognize the efforts of the entire team. Whether in public speeches, internal meetings, or everyday interactions, giving credit where it is due fosters a culture of appreciation and motivates people to continue working hard. It also serves as a reminder to the leader that their success is often the result of collective effort, not individual brilliance.

Seeking feedback regularly is another way for leaders to remain grounded and avoid arrogance. Leaders who actively ask for feedback from their teams, peers, and mentors demonstrate that they are open to growth and improvement. This practice not only helps leaders stay aware of areas where they can improve but also fosters a sense of inclusion, making people feel that their opinions are valued. Whether through formal feedback systems like surveys and reviews or informal conversations, leaders who seek input show that they are not above learning from others. Omar ibn al-Khattab was known for consulting with his companions before making important decisions, recognizing the wisdom of others, and ensuring that his leadership was informed by a diversity of perspectives. Modern leaders can emulate this by being open to constructive criticism and learning from those around them.

Another practical way to cultivate humility is by **leading through service**. This involves actively demonstrating that leadership is about serving the needs of others rather than commanding authority from above. Leaders who take on tasks that may seem "beneath" their role show that no job is too small or insignificant. In the business world, this might mean stepping into frontline roles during busy periods or showing a willingness to help wherever needed. In government, it could involve engaging with the community and participating in public service initiatives. When leaders make it clear that their role is to support and uplift others, it reinforces the idea that leadership is about service, not power.

Practicing empathy is another cornerstone of humility in leadership. Leaders who regularly put themselves in the shoes of others—whether employees, customers, or community members—are better able to understand the impact of their decisions. Empathy allows leaders to lead with compassion, ensuring that their choices take into account the well-being of others. This can be particularly important when making difficult or unpopular decisions. By demonstrating that they have considered the perspectives and feelings of those affected, leaders build trust and demonstrate that they are acting with the collective good in mind, rather than for personal gain or convenience.

Finally, modern leaders can cultivate humility by **keeping their ego in check and remaining focused on the bigger picture**. Leadership positions often come with praise, recognition, and influence, which can sometimes inflate a leader's sense of self-importance. To avoid this, leaders should remind themselves regularly that their role is temporary and that they are ultimately working toward a greater goal that transcends personal accolades. Keeping the focus on the mission or purpose of the organization or community helps leaders stay grounded and prevents them from being swayed by the trappings of power.

In conclusion, humility is not a trait that comes naturally to everyone, especially in positions of authority, but it is one that can be cultivated through conscious practice. By staying connected to the people they serve, admitting mistakes, sharing credit, seeking feedback, leading through service, practicing empathy, and focusing on the bigger picture, modern leaders can develop the humility needed to lead effectively. Omar ibn al-Khattab's life provides a timeless example of how humility can enhance leadership and ensure that power is used for the benefit of others, not for personal gain. Through these practical steps, today's leaders can avoid the arrogance that so often accompanies power and instead foster a leadership style that is grounded in respect, empathy, and service.

Chapter 3: Respect for Diversity: Omar ibn al-Khattab's Legacy of Inclusion

One of the defining features of Omar ibn al-Khattab's (may Allah be pleased with him) leadership was his remarkable respect for diversity, particularly his treatment of non-Muslims under Islamic rule. At a time when religious differences often led to conflict and division, Omar set a powerful example of tolerance and inclusion. His leadership was not only about expanding the Islamic empire but also about ensuring that all communities, regardless of their faith or background, were treated with fairness, respect, and dignity. Omar's approach to diversity offers important lessons for modern leaders, especially in a world that is increasingly interconnected and multicultural.

Perhaps the most notable example of Omar's respect for religious diversity occurred during the peaceful conquest of Jerusalem in 637 CE. After the city surrendered to the Muslim forces, Omar personally traveled to Jerusalem to finalize the terms of surrender. When he arrived, he met with the Christian Patriarch Sophronius, who feared the destruction of Christian religious sites and persecution of Christians under Muslim rule. Omar, however, reassured him and guaranteed the safety of Christian churches, including the revered Church of the Holy Sepulchre. He ensured that Christians would be free to practice their faith and that their places of worship would remain protected under Muslim governance.

One famous incident highlights Omar's deep respect for other religions. During his visit to Jerusalem, the time for prayer came while he was in the Church of the Holy Sepulchre. The Patriarch invited Omar to pray inside the church, but Omar respectfully declined. Instead, he prayed outside, explaining that if he had prayed inside, future generations of Muslims might take it as a reason to convert the church into a mosque. His refusal was a profound gesture of respect for the sanctity of the Christian site and an acknowledgment of the importance of preserving religious diversity.

Omar's leadership extended beyond the protection of religious sites; he implemented policies that safeguarded the rights of non-Muslims living under Islamic rule. The **Pact of Umar**, a set of guidelines attributed to him, outlined the rights and responsibilities of non-Muslims (Dhimmis) under Muslim rule. Non-Muslims were allowed to practice their religion freely, maintain their places of worship, and live according to their own religious laws. In return, they paid the **jizya** (a tax in exchange for protection), which exempted them from military service. This system created an atmosphere of mutual respect and coexistence, allowing different religious communities to thrive within the Islamic state.

For modern leaders, Omar's example provides a critical lesson in how tolerance and inclusion can create a harmonious society. In today's increasingly diverse world, where communities are often made up of people from various religious, ethnic, and cultural backgrounds, leaders must prioritize the protection of minority rights and promote inclusiveness. Omar's ability to lead a diverse empire without marginalizing non-Muslim communities demonstrates that diversity, when respected, can be a source of strength rather than division.

Tolerance and inclusion are essential for building a society where people feel safe, valued, and able to contribute meaningfully. When leaders show respect for diversity, they foster unity by ensuring that everyone, regardless of their background, feels they have a place in the community. This creates an environment where differences are not feared but embraced, allowing for greater cooperation and understanding between different groups.

In today's political and social landscape, leaders can promote diversity by implementing **policies that protect the rights of minorities and marginalized groups**. Ensuring that everyone has equal access to opportunities, resources, and protections under the law is key to maintaining social harmony. Leaders should work to create laws that prevent discrimination based on race, religion, ethnicity, gender, or any other characteristic. Just as Omar ensured that Christians and Jews could practice their faith freely under Islamic rule, modern leaders must protect the religious and cultural rights of all groups, particularly in multicultural societies.

Another important step modern leaders can take is to **create inclusive spaces for dialogue** between different communities. Omar's ability to work directly with leaders of other faiths, such as Patriarch Sophronius, demonstrated the importance of open communication and mutual respect. Modern leaders can facilitate interfaith and intercultural dialogue, encouraging communities to come together and learn from one another. This not only helps to break down stereotypes and misunderstandings but also fosters a spirit of collaboration and peace.

Leaders can also promote diversity by **building diverse teams and leadership structures** within their organizations or governments. A diverse leadership team brings a variety of perspectives and experiences to the table, helping to create more informed and balanced decision-making. By including voices from different backgrounds, leaders can ensure that policies and decisions reflect the needs of the entire community, not just a select few. This inclusiveness helps to create a more equitable society where all individuals feel represented.

Omar's legacy teaches modern leaders that true strength lies in the ability to unite diverse groups of people under a common goal of justice and fairness. His respect for religious diversity and his efforts to protect minority rights created a stable and harmonious society that flourished under his leadership. In an increasingly globalized world, where diversity is often seen as a source of division, leaders must adopt an inclusive approach that celebrates differences and protects the rights of all individuals, regardless of their background.

In conclusion, Omar ibn al-Khattab's treatment of non-Muslims and his respect for religious diversity offer timeless lessons for modern leaders. His policies of inclusion and protection for minority rights demonstrate that tolerance and respect are the foundations of a peaceful and prosperous society. By promoting diversity, protecting minority rights, and fostering dialogue between different communities, modern leaders can create environments where everyone feels valued and able to contribute. Omar's leadership shows that true greatness lies not in asserting dominance but in creating a society where all people, regardless of their differences, can live together in peace and harmony.

Omar's Respect for Religious Diversity: Protecting Non-Muslims in Jerusalem

OMAR IBN AL-KHATTAB'S (may Allah be pleased with him) leadership is remembered for many qualities, but one of the most striking is his respect for religious diversity, especially in his treatment of non-Muslims. As the caliph of a rapidly expanding Islamic empire, Omar had the responsibility to govern over a population that included people of various faiths. His commitment to justice and fairness extended beyond the Muslim community, and this was most notably demonstrated in his protection of Christian sites and his respectful treatment of non-Muslims in Jerusalem.

In 637 CE, after the peaceful conquest of Jerusalem, Omar traveled to the city to finalize its surrender. This moment was crucial, as Jerusalem was a religiously significant city, not only for Muslims but also for Christians and Jews. The Christian Patriarch of Jerusalem,

Sophronius, met with Omar, fearing that Muslim rule would lead to the destruction of Christian churches and persecution of Christians. However, Omar's response was one of reassurance and protection. He guaranteed the safety of all Christian holy sites, including the Church of the Holy Sepulchre, one of the most sacred sites in Christendom. He allowed the Christian population to continue practicing their faith freely and without fear.

One of the most telling moments of Omar's respect for religious diversity occurred when the time for prayer came during his visit to the Church of the Holy Sepulchre. The Patriarch invited Omar to pray inside the church, but Omar respectfully declined. Instead, he chose to pray outside the church. When asked why, Omar explained that if he had prayed inside, future generations of Muslims might use his actions as a justification to convert the church into a mosque. His decision to pray outside was a profound act of respect for the Christian site, ensuring its sanctity and protecting it from future encroachment. This gesture reflected Omar's deep understanding of the importance of preserving religious diversity and respecting the beliefs of others.

Beyond his personal actions, Omar also established policies that protected the rights of non-Muslims under Islamic rule. The **Pact of Umar**, attributed to his governance, laid out the guidelines for how non-Muslims (Dhimmis) were to be treated in the Islamic state. According to the pact, non-Muslims were allowed to practice their religion freely, maintain their places of worship, and live according to their religious laws. In return, they paid the **jizya**, a tax that exempted them from military service and provided them protection by the Muslim state. This arrangement created a system of coexistence where non-Muslims could thrive under Muslim rule, contributing to the stability and prosperity of the empire.

Omar's protection of non-Muslim religious sites extended beyond Jerusalem. Throughout the Islamic empire, he ensured that Christian and Jewish places of worship were preserved and respected. His policies reflected a broader principle of justice that applied to all people, regardless of their faith. Omar's respect for religious diversity was not just a political tactic but a deeply rooted belief in the importance of fairness and inclusiveness. By safeguarding the rights of non-Muslims, Omar set a precedent for future Islamic rulers, demonstrating that religious tolerance was a core value of Islamic governance.

Omar's treatment of non-Muslims was also a reflection of Islamic teachings. The Qur'an emphasizes the importance of respecting people of other faiths and protecting their rights. Omar, as a devout Muslim, embodied these principles in his leadership. His commitment to justice extended to everyone under his rule, and he made it clear that Islam was not a religion of compulsion or oppression. By allowing non-Muslims to live in peace and protecting their religious practices, Omar reinforced the idea that Islam values coexistence and mutual respect.

The policies and actions of Omar ibn al-Khattab in Jerusalem and throughout the Islamic empire had far-reaching implications. His leadership created an environment where religious diversity was not only tolerated but protected. This respect for different faiths contributed to the stability of the empire, as non-Muslim communities felt secure under Muslim rule. They were able to maintain their religious and cultural identities while participating in the broader society. This model of governance, where multiple religious communities coexisted peacefully, became one of the hallmarks of Islamic civilization during the Rashidun and later periods.

In today's world, where religious intolerance and conflict often dominate headlines, Omar's respect for religious diversity offers a powerful lesson in how leaders can promote peace and unity through inclusiveness. His actions in Jerusalem stand as a timeless example of how true leadership requires not only strength and vision but also empathy and respect for the beliefs of others. By ensuring that Christian sites were protected and allowing non-Muslims to practice their faith freely, Omar showed that diversity is not a weakness but a strength that can contribute to the prosperity and stability of society.

Omar ibn al-Khattab's treatment of non-Muslims, particularly his protection of Christian sites in Jerusalem, is a testament to his commitment to justice and fairness for all. His respect for religious diversity was a reflection of his broader belief in the importance of serving all people, regardless of their faith or background. His leadership set a standard for tolerance and inclusion that has resonated throughout Islamic history, offering valuable lessons for leaders today on the importance of protecting minority rights and fostering harmony in diverse societies.

The Power of Tolerance and Inclusion in Building a Harmonious Society

IN A WORLD THAT IS increasingly interconnected and diverse, the ability of leaders to embrace tolerance and inclusion is more critical than ever. Omar ibn al-Khattab (may Allah be pleased with him) provides a timeless example of how tolerance can be a powerful tool for fostering peace, stability, and unity. His leadership, especially his respect for non-Muslim communities under Islamic rule, demonstrated that embracing diversity can strengthen a society rather than divide it. For modern leaders, the lessons from Omar's rule highlight the essential role that tolerance and inclusion play in building harmonious societies where all individuals, regardless of their background, feel valued and respected.

Tolerance, as demonstrated by Omar, is more than just allowing people to coexist. It requires actively protecting the rights of others, particularly those in the minority, and ensuring that their beliefs and practices are respected. In Jerusalem, for example, Omar safeguarded Christian religious sites and allowed Christians to practice their faith freely. His decision to refrain from praying inside the Church of the

Holy Sepulchre, even when invited, was a significant gesture of respect for another faith's sacred space. By protecting the religious rights of non-Muslims, Omar fostered a sense of security and inclusion, which in turn strengthened the unity of the diverse population under his rule.

For modern leaders, the lesson is clear: tolerance is the foundation of trust within a society. When people feel that their beliefs and identities are respected, they are more likely to contribute positively to the community. In contrast, when certain groups are marginalized or discriminated against, it leads to resentment, division, and social unrest. Leaders who prioritize inclusion create an environment where differences are not just tolerated but celebrated as strengths. This inclusive mindset encourages collaboration and understanding among different groups, reducing the risk of conflict and promoting social cohesion.

Inclusion goes beyond tolerance by actively ensuring that all members of society, particularly those who may be marginalized, have equal access to opportunities and protections. Omar's governance system, which protected the rights of non-Muslims and allowed them to participate in the broader society, is a model of inclusion. By allowing religious minorities to maintain their traditions and live according to their own laws, while still contributing to the welfare of the Islamic state, Omar built a sense of shared responsibility and mutual respect. This approach to inclusion created a stable, harmonious society where diverse groups could coexist peacefully and productively.

Modern leaders can apply these principles by actively promoting policies that protect the rights of all citizens, regardless of their race, religion, or cultural background. This can take the form of anti-discrimination laws, inclusive hiring practices, or creating platforms for minority voices to be heard in decision-making processes. Leaders must recognize that inclusion is not a passive act but an active commitment to ensuring that all people have the opportunity to thrive.

When everyone feels they have a stake in the success of the society, it fosters unity and reduces divisions.

In addition to creating a more harmonious society, tolerance and inclusion have practical benefits for governance and organizational success. Diverse societies and teams bring together a wide range of perspectives, skills, and experiences, which can lead to more innovative solutions to problems. Leaders who embrace diversity and inclusion allow for a broader exchange of ideas and a more comprehensive approach to decision-making. This inclusiveness can be a source of strength in a globalized world, where complex challenges require input from a variety of perspectives.

Another important lesson for modern leaders is the role of **dialogue in promoting tolerance and inclusion**. Omar's respectful interactions with non-Muslim leaders, such as Patriarch Sophronius, exemplified how dialogue can bridge gaps between different communities. By engaging in open and honest communication, leaders can build trust and understanding across cultural or religious divides. This dialogue helps to break down stereotypes and prejudices, fostering empathy and cooperation between groups that may otherwise be in conflict. Modern leaders can take inspiration from Omar by encouraging interfaith and intercultural dialogue as a means of building bridges and promoting peace in diverse communities.

Finally, modern leaders must understand that promoting tolerance and inclusion is an ongoing effort. It requires vigilance and a consistent commitment to justice and fairness. Omar's policies towards non-Muslims, as outlined in the Pact of Umar, were not one-time actions but part of a broader governance strategy that ensured the protection and inclusion of minority communities throughout his rule. Similarly, modern leaders must continue to monitor and address issues of inequality or discrimination, ensuring that all groups are treated fairly and that no one is left behind.

In conclusion, Omar ibn al-Khattab's leadership provides a powerful lesson for modern leaders on the importance of tolerance and inclusion. By respecting the rights of all people, regardless of their background, and creating an environment where everyone can participate and thrive, leaders can build harmonious and prosperous societies. Tolerance fosters trust and unity, while inclusion ensures that everyone has a stake in the collective success of the community. Modern leaders who embrace these principles will not only create more stable and peaceful societies but also tap into the full potential of their diverse populations, leading to greater innovation, collaboration, and social progress.

Promoting Diversity and Protecting Minority Rights in Today's Political Landscape

IN TODAY'S INCREASINGLY diverse and interconnected world, leaders must actively promote diversity and protect the rights of minorities to ensure social harmony and equal opportunities for all. Achieving this requires a conscious effort to create inclusive policies, foster dialogue, and safeguard the rights of marginalized communities. Omar ibn al-Khattab's (may Allah be pleased with him) leadership provides a timeless example of how protecting religious and cultural diversity can lead to a stable and prosperous society. For modern leaders, applying these principles involves taking specific, actionable steps to promote diversity and inclusion in the political landscape.

The first step in promoting diversity is to **create and enforce laws that protect against discrimination**. In many societies, minority groups face discrimination based on race, religion, ethnicity, gender, or sexual orientation. Modern leaders can take inspiration from Omar's governance, where non-Muslims were granted rights and protections under Islamic rule. Leaders today must ensure that anti-discrimination laws are in place and rigorously enforced to prevent unequal treatment in areas such as employment, education, housing, and public services. These laws should cover both direct discrimination and systemic inequalities that disproportionately affect minority communities.

In addition to legal protections, **representation matters**. Leaders must ensure that minority groups are represented in government, decision-making bodies, and leadership positions within public and private institutions. Diverse representation ensures that the interests and concerns of all communities are considered and addressed. By including individuals from various backgrounds in policymaking processes, leaders can make more informed and inclusive decisions that benefit everyone, not just the majority. This can involve setting up advisory councils that include representatives from minority communities or creating policies that encourage diversity in political appointments and leadership roles.

A key element of promoting diversity is to **encourage and facilitate dialogue between different cultural, religious, and ethnic groups**. Omar's respectful interactions with non-Muslim leaders, such as Patriarch Sophronius, illustrate the importance of communication and understanding across religious lines. In today's context, leaders can create platforms for interfaith and intercultural dialogue, allowing different communities to come together and address shared challenges. This could take the form of community forums, public discussions, or partnerships between religious and cultural organizations. Open dialogue helps to break down stereotypes, build trust, and promote mutual respect, making it easier to resolve conflicts and foster social cohesion.

Education also plays a critical role in promoting diversity and protecting minority rights. Leaders should work to ensure that educational curricula reflect the diversity of the society and include the histories and contributions of minority groups. This helps to foster a sense of belonging among all students and counteract ignorance or prejudice. Schools should be environments where diversity is celebrated and where students learn the value of inclusion from a young age. In addition, promoting language diversity, such as offering education in minority languages, can help preserve cultural identities while ensuring that minority groups are able to participate fully in society.

Economic inclusion is another crucial aspect of promoting diversity. Minority groups often face systemic barriers to economic participation, such as unequal access to job opportunities, capital, or housing. Modern leaders can address these issues by implementing policies that promote economic equity, such as equal employment opportunities, access to financial resources for minority-owned businesses, and affordable housing initiatives in minority communities. By removing economic barriers, leaders help ensure that everyone has the opportunity to contribute to and benefit from the economy, leading to greater social mobility and a more inclusive society.

Another important step is to **strengthen legal frameworks that protect the rights of minority groups**, particularly in terms of religious and cultural freedoms. Omar's protection of non-Muslim religious sites, such as Christian churches in Jerusalem, is a model for how leaders can safeguard the rights of religious minorities. In today's political landscape, leaders should work to ensure that religious minorities are free to practice their faith without fear of persecution or discrimination. This can include providing legal protections for religious practices, securing places of worship, and preventing hate crimes or religiously motivated violence. Protecting the rights of minorities also involves recognizing and upholding their cultural traditions and practices, which contribute to the overall richness of society.

Empowering minority communities is another essential step. Leaders should provide platforms and opportunities for minority groups to advocate for their rights and participate in the political process. This can involve supporting grassroots organizations, funding initiatives that benefit minority communities, and ensuring that political processes are accessible to all, including through language services and outreach efforts. By empowering minority groups to engage with and influence the political system, leaders promote a more inclusive and representative democracy.

Lastly, modern leaders must **demonstrate accountability and transparency** in their efforts to promote diversity and protect minority rights. This means regularly assessing the effectiveness of diversity policies and being open to feedback from minority communities. Leaders should be willing to make changes based on that feedback and be transparent about the steps they are taking to address issues of inequality or discrimination. Publicly committing to diversity goals and providing regular reports on progress helps build trust with minority communities and ensures that leaders remain accountable to their commitments.

In conclusion, promoting diversity and protecting minority rights requires proactive leadership and a commitment to justice and inclusion. By enacting and enforcing anti-discrimination laws, ensuring representation, fostering dialogue, supporting education, promoting economic equity, safeguarding religious and cultural freedoms, empowering minority communities, and maintaining transparency, modern leaders can build societies that are not only diverse but also harmonious and unified. Omar ibn al-Khattab's leadership serves as a lasting example of how respecting diversity can lead to a stronger, more resilient society where all individuals have the opportunity to thrive.

Part II: Accountability, Consultation, and Personal Discipline: The Pillars of Responsible Leadership

Leadership is not just about authority or decision-making; it is deeply rooted in responsibility, wisdom, and the ability to stay disciplined. Omar ibn al-Khattab (may Allah be pleased with him) embodied these principles throughout his time as caliph, setting a timeless example of what it means to lead with integrity, foresight, and devotion. His leadership style was shaped by a profound sense of accountability to the people he governed, a strong belief in collective wisdom through consultation, and a personal discipline rooted in faith and moral values. These qualities made him one of the most effective and respected leaders in history, and they offer crucial lessons for modern leaders who seek to lead with purpose and ethics.

Omar's leadership was characterized by an unwavering commitment to **accountability**. He held himself responsible not only for the decisions he made but for the well-being of every individual in his empire. His personal inspections of markets and his habit of walking the streets at night disguised as an ordinary man were clear demonstrations of his belief that a leader must be directly involved in the lives of the people he serves. This accountability created a culture of trust and transparency within his administration, ensuring that justice and fairness were upheld. For modern leaders, the lesson here is profound: true leadership is not about delegation alone but about personal involvement and responsibility. Leaders who hold themselves accountable are more likely to inspire trust and loyalty among their followers.

Consultation and collective decision-making were also key to Omar's leadership. He understood the importance of seeking counsel and valuing diverse opinions, and he regularly practiced *Shura*, or consultation, with his companions and advisors. This practice allowed him to make informed decisions that reflected the needs and wisdom of the broader community. One of the most notable examples of this was his appointment of a council to choose the next caliph after his death, ensuring that leadership succession would be handled through consultation rather than autocratic decision-making. Omar's reliance on collective wisdom shows that no leader has all the answers. Modern leaders can benefit from this by fostering open dialogue and collaboration, making sure that important decisions are made with input from those who represent various perspectives and areas of expertise.

Finally, Omar's leadership was underpinned by a deep sense of **personal discipline and devotion**. His life was marked by regular prayer, fasting, and acts of charity, which kept him grounded and focused on his core values. Despite his immense power, he never allowed himself to be swayed by the temptations of wealth or comfort. His self-discipline was not only a personal virtue but a guiding force in his leadership, ensuring that he remained steadfast in his principles and committed to serving the people. For modern leaders, this offers a valuable lesson: self-discipline and adherence to core values are essential for ethical and effective leadership. Leaders who practice self-discipline are more likely to inspire others through their actions and lead by example.

This section of the book delves into these foundational aspects of leadership—accountability, consultation, and personal discipline—and explores how modern leaders can apply these principles in their own governance and decision-making processes. By examining Omar's practices, we uncover the timeless wisdom behind his approach and how these qualities can foster responsible, ethical, and effective leadership in today's world. Through personal accountability, the use of collective wisdom, and the development of self-discipline, leaders can create a legacy of integrity and trust, just as Omar did centuries ago.

Chapter 4: Accountability and Responsibility: Omar's Commitment to His People

One of the most defining aspects of Omar ibn al-Khattab's (may Allah be pleased with him) leadership was his unwavering commitment to accountability. Unlike many rulers throughout history who remained distant from the people they governed, Omar made it a point to personally involve himself in the lives of those under his rule. He did not view leadership as a means of exerting authority from a position of comfort but as a responsibility to ensure the well-being and fairness of society. His personal inspections of markets, nighttime walks, and efforts to address the concerns of ordinary people set a powerful precedent for how leaders should hold themselves accountable for the welfare of their people.

Omar's accountability was rooted in his deep belief that a leader is responsible not just for the major decisions of governance but also for the small, everyday issues that affect the lives of individuals. He would often walk the streets of Medina at night, disguised, to observe firsthand how people were living. During these walks, he would listen to the concerns of the people and address injustices or hardships that may not have been brought to his attention through official channels. One of the most famous stories tells of how Omar overheard a woman in distress, struggling to provide food for her children. Moved by her plight, he immediately took action, delivering food to her family himself. This level of personal involvement reflected his profound sense of responsibility toward his people, ensuring that no one was left neglected or mistreated.

In addition to his nighttime patrols, Omar regularly inspected the markets, ensuring that traders were conducting business fairly and that no one was being cheated or exploited. He believed that economic justice was central to the well-being of the community and that it was his duty to ensure that trade was conducted in a just manner. His presence in the markets was a deterrent to those who might have been tempted to engage in dishonest practices, knowing that the caliph himself was watching and enforcing fairness. Omar's active involvement in these areas demonstrates his understanding that leadership is not just about issuing orders but about being directly accountable for the outcomes of those decisions.

For modern leaders, the lesson from Omar's life is clear: accountability is not a passive responsibility, but an active, ongoing commitment. Leaders must not distance themselves from the people they serve, but instead make a conscious effort to engage with them, understand their needs, and take responsibility for their well-being. Accountability in leadership builds trust and respect, as people are more likely to follow leaders who they know are genuinely concerned with their welfare. When leaders hold themselves accountable, they create an environment of transparency and integrity that permeates throughout the organization or society they lead.

In today's political and corporate landscapes, practicing accountability and transparency requires leaders to be open about their decisions, actions, and mistakes. One of the ways modern leaders can practice accountability is through **open communication**. Leaders should regularly update the public or their teams about the reasons behind their decisions, allowing others to understand the thought process and objectives behind those choices. Whether it's a new policy or a strategic business decision, transparency in decision-making helps create trust. When people are informed, they are more likely to feel included and more willing to support the leader's vision.

Another practical way to implement accountability is through **public engagement and feedback mechanisms**. Just as Omar walked the streets and listened to the concerns of his people, modern leaders can create opportunities for direct interaction with those they serve. This can take the form of town hall meetings, open forums, or digital platforms where feedback is encouraged and taken seriously. By engaging directly with the public or employees, leaders show that they value input and are willing to listen to concerns, criticisms, and suggestions. This openness can prevent issues from escalating and allows for more proactive governance or management.

Setting clear expectations and standards is another way leaders can ensure accountability. By establishing clear guidelines for behavior, performance, and ethics, leaders create a framework for accountability that applies to everyone within the organization or society. This includes setting personal accountability for their own actions, holding themselves to the same standards they expect of others. When leaders lead by example and demonstrate that no one, not even those at the highest level, is above accountability, it fosters a culture of responsibility and fairness.

Lastly, leaders must be **willing to admit mistakes and take corrective action** when necessary. Accountability is not about perfection; it's about honesty and integrity. Omar was known for admitting his mistakes and immediately rectifying them. Modern leaders can apply this by owning up to errors or poor decisions, openly discussing how they plan to fix the problem, and ensuring that such mistakes are not repeated. This level of transparency not only builds trust but also demonstrates that accountability is a priority, even when things go wrong.

In conclusion, accountability and responsibility are the cornerstones of ethical leadership. Omar ibn al-Khattab's personal involvement in the lives of his people, his commitment to fairness in markets, and his active engagement with the public provide a timeless model for how leaders should hold themselves accountable. For modern leaders, the path to accountability involves direct engagement, transparency in decision-making, setting clear standards, and the courage to admit mistakes. By embracing these practices, leaders can create a culture of trust, integrity, and responsibility that strengthens their leadership and benefits the people they serve.

Omar's Personal Accountability: A Leader Among the People

OMAR IBN AL-KHATTAB (may Allah be pleased with him) set a powerful example of what it means to be accountable as a leader. His sense of responsibility for the well-being of his people extended far beyond issuing orders or implementing policies; it was a deeply personal commitment to ensuring justice, fairness, and the basic needs of every individual under his rule. Omar did not lead from a distance or isolate himself from the struggles of the people. Instead, he made it a point to be present, involved, and attentive to the everyday lives of the citizens. His regular inspections of markets and nightly walks through the streets are two of the most famous examples of his personal accountability, reflecting a leadership style that was built on direct engagement and genuine concern for the welfare of his community.

One of Omar's most notable practices was his habit of **walking the streets of Medina at night**, often disguised, so that he could observe the true conditions of his people. During these nightly patrols, Omar would listen for signs of distress or hardship, often without revealing his identity. He understood that the official reports he received might not capture the full reality of life for ordinary citizens, so he took it upon himself to witness their struggles firsthand. By walking among the people, he was able to uncover hidden injustices or unmet needs that might have gone unnoticed. This practice reflected his belief that a leader must be directly accountable for the well-being of all, even those who might otherwise feel voiceless or forgotten.

One famous story from these nighttime walks involves a widow who was struggling to feed her children. Omar, passing by her home, overheard her complaining to herself about the lack of food and her inability to care for her children. Deeply moved, Omar returned to the treasury, collected food, and carried it himself to the woman's home. When one of his companions offered to carry the load for him, Omar replied, "Will you carry my burden on the Day of Judgment?" This story highlights not only his sense of personal accountability but also his deep empathy and understanding that leadership is not just about ruling—it is about ensuring the well-being of every individual, especially the vulnerable.

Omar's personal involvement in the lives of his people did not end with his nighttime patrols. He also took a proactive role in **inspecting the markets of Medina**, ensuring that traders and merchants conducted their business fairly and without deceit. As a caliph, Omar recognized that economic justice was central to the well-being of the community. He wanted to ensure that no one was being cheated, and that people were able to buy and sell goods at fair prices. His presence in the marketplace acted as a deterrent against dishonest practices and gave the people confidence that they were being protected from exploitation. Omar's inspections of the markets showed that accountability for the well-being of the people extended even into the economic sphere, where fairness and justice had to be upheld.

During these inspections, Omar was known for his direct and hands-on approach. He did not simply rely on others to report problems; he investigated them personally. If he saw something unjust, he would confront it immediately, regardless of who was involved. He famously confronted merchants who attempted to manipulate prices or sell inferior goods. In these moments, Omar demonstrated that no one—whether wealthy merchant or common citizen—was above the law or beyond the reach of justice. His willingness to step into the marketplace and enforce fairness underscored his commitment to accountability at every level of society.

Omar's practice of holding himself accountable was not limited to economic or social matters. He also took responsibility for the governance of his officials and the execution of laws. He appointed governors to oversee various regions of the growing Islamic empire, but he did not simply leave them to rule without oversight. Omar regularly corresponded with them, ensuring that they upheld the values of justice and fairness that he embodied. If a governor acted unjustly, Omar did not hesitate to remove them from power, no matter how influential they were. This reinforced the idea that leadership is a trust and that those in power must answer to the people and to Allah.

Omar's personal accountability extended to his own actions and decisions as well. He was known for his humility in leadership, often seeking the advice of others and openly admitting his mistakes. He understood that even as a caliph, he was not infallible and that his decisions had a direct impact on the lives of the people. His famous quote, "If a mule were to stumble on the banks of the Euphrates, I would fear that Allah would hold me accountable for not having leveled the road for it," exemplifies the depth of his sense of responsibility. He believed that even the smallest oversight could have significant consequences, and as such, he held himself to the highest standards of accountability.

In conclusion, Omar's personal accountability was one of the hallmarks of his leadership. His nightly walks, market inspections, and constant engagement with his people demonstrated his deep commitment to ensuring justice and fairness for all. He did not see leadership as a distant or isolated position but as a responsibility that required direct involvement in the lives of those he served. For Omar, accountability was not just a principle; it was a daily practice that defined his leadership. His actions remind modern leaders that true leadership involves more than authority—it requires personal accountability, empathy, and a relentless commitment to the welfare of the people.

The Importance of Accountability: Why Leaders Must Be Responsible for the Welfare of Their People

ACCOUNTABILITY IS A fundamental aspect of ethical and effective leadership. A leader's responsibility extends beyond making decisions or setting policies; it involves ensuring that the people under their care are treated fairly, that their needs are met, and that justice prevails in every aspect of society. Omar ibn al-Khattab (may Allah be pleased with him) exemplified this principle through his constant engagement with the people, his personal involvement in their daily lives, and his unwavering commitment to fairness. His leadership shows that when leaders hold themselves accountable, they build trust, inspire loyalty, and create a stable and just society.

For modern leaders, accountability is crucial because it establishes a foundation of trust between the leader and the people. When leaders demonstrate that they are accountable for their actions, the public feels confident that their concerns and needs are being addressed. This trust is essential for maintaining social cohesion and stability. Leaders who are accountable do not isolate themselves from the people they serve; instead, they actively engage with them, listen to their concerns, and take responsibility for the outcomes of their decisions. This transparency reassures people that their leaders are working in their best interest and are not disconnected from their realities.

Accountability also strengthens the **legitimacy of leadership**. When leaders openly take responsibility for their actions, they reinforce their credibility and integrity. This is especially important in times of crisis or uncertainty, when public confidence in leadership can waver. Leaders who hold themselves accountable demonstrate that they are willing to stand by their decisions, admit mistakes, and correct them when necessary. This willingness to be transparent about both successes and failures builds respect and shows that the leader values honesty and justice over self-preservation or image management.

Omar's leadership serves as a timeless example of this principle. By regularly inspecting markets and walking the streets of Medina, Omar made himself directly accountable to the people, ensuring that no injustice went unnoticed. He was willing to correct unfair practices immediately, regardless of who was involved, and he did not hesitate to rectify mistakes when they were brought to his attention. This direct involvement showed the people that Omar was not only aware of their struggles but actively working to alleviate them. Modern leaders can learn from this by recognizing that accountability is not a passive act but a proactive and ongoing commitment to justice.

Another reason why accountability is so important is that it helps to **prevent abuses of power**. When leaders are not held accountable, they may be tempted to act in their own self-interest rather than in the interest of the people they serve. This can lead to corruption, exploitation, and a breakdown in the social order. By holding themselves accountable and ensuring that they are answerable to the public, leaders set a standard of integrity that discourages unethical behavior and fosters a culture of responsibility within the organization or society they lead.

Furthermore, accountability ensures that leaders remain connected to the realities of the people they govern. When leaders take responsibility for the well-being of their people, they are more likely to engage with them directly, as Omar did, and better understand their needs and challenges. This understanding allows leaders to make more informed decisions that reflect the true needs of the community, rather than relying solely on reports or distant assessments. Accountability, therefore, not only strengthens the relationship between leaders and the people but also leads to more effective governance, as decisions are made with a deeper understanding of the people's experiences.

Leaders who practice accountability also serve as **role models** for others. When leaders demonstrate that they are responsible for their actions and the well-being of their people, they inspire others to act with integrity and responsibility. This creates a culture of accountability that extends throughout the organization or society, where people at all levels take responsibility for their actions and work to ensure that justice and fairness are upheld. Omar's leadership set such a precedent, as he held not only himself but also his governors and officials accountable for their actions, ensuring that justice was maintained across the empire.

In conclusion, accountability is a cornerstone of ethical leadership. Modern leaders must recognize that they are responsible for the welfare of their people, not only in terms of governance but in ensuring justice, fairness, and the protection of rights. By holding themselves accountable, leaders build trust, prevent abuses of power, remain connected to the people's needs, and set a positive example for others to follow. Omar ibn al-Khattab's leadership demonstrates the profound impact of accountability in creating a just and harmonious society, and modern leaders would do well to embrace this principle in their own leadership practices.

Practicing Accountability and Transparency in Modern Governance

IN TODAY'S COMPLEX and interconnected world, accountability and transparency are essential elements of effective leadership. When leaders are open about their actions and decisions and hold themselves responsible for the outcomes, they build trust, foster stability, and ensure the long-term success of their governance. Omar ibn al-Khattab (may Allah be pleased with him) practiced these principles by staying engaged with the people, addressing their concerns directly, and ensuring that justice was upheld. For modern leaders, adopting similar practices can help create a culture of accountability and transparency that strengthens governance and inspires public confidence.

The first step for modern leaders to practice accountability is to **establish clear communication channels with the public or the people they serve**. Leaders should regularly inform citizens or employees about the decisions being made, the reasons behind those decisions, and the expected outcomes. This can be done through public addresses, town hall meetings, or digital platforms where leaders engage directly with the people. When leaders explain their actions and policies in an open and accessible way, they reduce uncertainty and build trust. People are more likely to support a leader's vision when they understand the rationale behind the decisions and feel that they are part of the process.

Leaders can also **promote transparency by providing access to data and information** about government or organizational operations. By making financial records, policy decisions, and performance metrics available to the public, leaders demonstrate that they have nothing to hide. This kind of transparency not only increases accountability but also invites public scrutiny, which can help identify areas where improvements can be made. Public transparency can be facilitated through regular reports, online dashboards, or open data initiatives that allow people to track the progress of projects, budget allocations, or other key governance metrics.

Another crucial element of accountability is **creating systems of checks and balances**. Leaders must ensure that there are mechanisms in place to hold them, as well as their officials or team members, accountable for their actions. This can involve independent oversight bodies, ethics committees, or internal audits that regularly review decisions and policies to ensure they align with ethical standards and public interests. Omar's willingness to remove governors who acted unjustly illustrates the importance of oversight in maintaining accountability. In modern governance, leaders should establish and support independent institutions that can objectively evaluate their performance and address any misuse of power.

Encouraging public participation in decision-making is another effective way to promote accountability. Leaders can create platforms for citizens to voice their opinions, provide feedback, and participate in discussions on important issues. Public consultations, referendums, or advisory councils made up of diverse community members can help ensure that decisions reflect the needs and priorities of the people. By actively listening to and incorporating the input of those they serve, leaders demonstrate that they are accountable to the public and committed to making decisions that benefit everyone, not just a select few.

A critical aspect of accountability is the **willingness to admit mistakes and correct them**. Leaders must be prepared to take responsibility when things go wrong and communicate openly about how they plan to fix the problem. Omar's readiness to rectify injustices when they were brought to his attention is an important example of how leaders can show accountability by acknowledging their errors. Modern leaders should foster a culture where mistakes are not hidden or deflected but addressed openly and resolved through corrective action. Admitting mistakes builds credibility, as it shows that leaders are focused on the greater good rather than protecting their reputation.

Additionally, leaders can practice accountability by **setting clear goals and regularly measuring performance against those goals**. Leaders should establish benchmarks for success and provide regular updates on progress. This level of transparency ensures that people can see whether the leader is delivering on their promises and where adjustments may need to be made. When leaders are clear about their objectives and hold themselves accountable for achieving them, they foster trust and demonstrate their commitment to effective governance.

Finally, modern leaders can **lead by example** in their personal conduct. Just as Omar held himself to high moral and ethical standards, modern leaders must embody the principles of accountability and transparency in their everyday actions. Leaders who show integrity, admit faults, and demonstrate accountability in their personal and professional lives set the tone for the entire organization or government. By modeling the behavior they expect from others, leaders inspire a culture of responsibility and transparency that permeates all levels of governance.

In conclusion, practicing accountability and transparency is essential for modern leaders to build trust, maintain public confidence, and ensure effective governance. Through open communication, access to information, systems of checks and balances, public participation, willingness to admit mistakes, setting clear goals, and leading by example, leaders can create a culture of accountability that strengthens their leadership and benefits society as a whole. Omar ibn al-Khattab's leadership provides a timeless model of how accountability can lead to just and effective governance, and modern leaders can draw on these principles to enhance their own practices.

Chapter 5: Consultation and Wisdom: The Practice of Shura in Leadership

One of the most remarkable aspects of Omar ibn al-Khattab's (may Allah be pleased with him) leadership was his consistent use of *Shura*, or consultation, as a guiding principle in decision-making. Unlike autocratic rulers who relied solely on their own judgment, Omar actively sought the advice and counsel of those around him, believing in the value of collective wisdom. This approach was not only a reflection of his humility but also a strategic method to ensure that decisions were made with a full understanding of the issues at hand. His practice of Shura demonstrated the power of open dialogue and collaboration, emphasizing that leadership is most effective when it involves the contributions and perspectives of others.

Omar's practice of Shura is perhaps best exemplified in his decision to appoint a council to choose his successor as caliph. As his health began to decline, Omar recognized the importance of ensuring a smooth and fair transition of power. Instead of selecting a successor unilaterally, he appointed a council of six respected companions to deliberate and select the next caliph. This decision reflected his belief that leadership should not be imposed by one individual but should emerge from thoughtful consultation and collective agreement. By involving trusted individuals in the decision-making process, Omar ensured that the future leadership would have legitimacy and broad support within the community.

Omar's use of Shura extended to many aspects of his leadership, from matters of governance and military strategy to social and economic policies. He regularly sought advice from a range of people, including scholars, military commanders, and ordinary citizens, recognizing that no single person could possess all the knowledge and insight necessary to lead effectively. His reliance on consultation allowed him to make more informed and balanced decisions, reflecting the needs and concerns of the wider community. This approach also reinforced the idea that leadership is a shared responsibility, with input from different perspectives contributing to the overall success of the decision.

For modern leaders, the lesson from Omar's use of Shura is clear: collective wisdom is a powerful tool for effective decision-making. Leaders who involve others in the decision-making process are more likely to arrive at solutions that are well-rounded, inclusive, and reflective of the diverse needs of the people they serve. By consulting others, leaders not only gain valuable insights but also foster a sense of ownership and collaboration among those involved. When people feel that their voices have been heard and that they have contributed to the decision-making process, they are more likely to support the outcomes and work toward their implementation.

Building a culture of consultation and open dialogue is particularly important in today's world, where the challenges leaders face are complex and multifaceted. No leader, no matter how experienced or knowledgeable, can have all the answers. By seeking the counsel of others, modern leaders can tap into a wealth of knowledge, expertise, and perspectives that they may not have access to on their own. This not only enhances the quality of decision-making but also helps to prevent blind spots or biases that could otherwise lead to poor outcomes.

One of the practical ways modern leaders can build a culture of collaboration is by **creating formal and informal mechanisms for consultation**. This could involve establishing advisory boards, councils, or committees that include representatives from different sectors, communities, or areas of expertise. These groups can provide valuable input on key decisions, ensuring that a range of voices are heard before a final decision is made. In addition to formal structures, leaders can encourage informal dialogue by fostering a culture where employees, team members, or citizens feel comfortable sharing their ideas and opinions without fear of retribution. By making consultation a regular part of the decision-making process, leaders create an environment of openness and trust.

Encouraging diversity of thought is another important aspect of building a collaborative leadership culture. Omar's practice of Shura included seeking advice from people with different backgrounds and perspectives, understanding that diversity of thought leads to more comprehensive and effective solutions. Modern leaders should actively seek out diverse voices, ensuring that their teams or advisory groups reflect a broad range of experiences, expertise, and viewpoints. This diversity helps to prevent groupthink, where everyone agrees on the same solution without fully exploring alternative options. By encouraging differing opinions and challenging assumptions, leaders can arrive at more innovative and well-considered decisions.

Leaders can also **facilitate open dialogue by creating safe spaces for discussion**. In many organizations or governments, people may hesitate to share their true thoughts or concerns for fear of backlash or criticism. Omar's leadership demonstrated that consultation only works when people feel empowered to speak freely and honestly. Modern leaders can create this environment by fostering a culture of respect and encouraging open communication at all levels. This could involve regular meetings where team members are encouraged to share their thoughts, feedback mechanisms that allow for anonymous input, or leadership retreats focused on brainstorming and collaborative problem-solving.

Another key to practicing Shura is for leaders to **remain humble and open to feedback**. Omar understood that consultation was not just about going through the motions but about genuinely valuing the input of others. He often adjusted his decisions based on the advice he received, demonstrating that a leader must be willing to listen, learn, and sometimes change course. Modern leaders can practice this by being open to feedback and showing that they are willing to adjust their strategies or policies based on the insights of others. This humility not only strengthens the decision-making process but also builds trust and respect among those being led.

In conclusion, Omar ibn al-Khattab's practice of Shura offers a powerful model for modern leadership. By embracing consultation and collective wisdom, leaders can make more informed, balanced, and effective decisions. Modern leaders can apply these principles by creating structures for collaboration, encouraging diverse viewpoints, facilitating open dialogue, and remaining open to feedback. Through consultation, leaders can build stronger, more inclusive teams and communities, ensuring that decisions are made with the input and support of those who will be affected by them. This approach not only leads to better outcomes but also fosters a culture of trust, respect, and shared responsibility in leadership.

Omar's Practice of Shura: Collective Wisdom in Decision-Making

OMAR IBN AL-KHATTAB (may Allah be pleased with him) was a leader who deeply understood the value of consultation, known in Islamic tradition as *Shura*. His approach to leadership was not driven by a sense of personal authority but by the belief that wisdom is best achieved through collective deliberation. This practice of seeking advice from others and involving key individuals in decision-making was a hallmark of his rule and is perhaps best illustrated by his decision to appoint a council to choose his successor as caliph. Omar's use of

Shura demonstrated his humility, his trust in the wisdom of others, and his commitment to justice in leadership.

Throughout his caliphate, Omar frequently consulted with his advisors and companions, valuing their opinions and insights. Whether the matter at hand was related to governance, economic policies, or military strategy, Omar understood that decisions made in isolation could be prone to error or bias. His practice of Shura ensured that important decisions were made with input from those who had diverse perspectives and expertise. By involving others, Omar fostered a sense of shared responsibility and collaboration, knowing that collective wisdom would lead to more balanced and effective governance.

One of the most notable examples of Omar's use of Shura occurred as he approached the end of his life. Recognizing that his time as caliph was coming to an end, Omar knew that the Muslim community needed a clear and just process for selecting his successor. Rather than appointing a successor unilaterally, as he had the power to do, Omar chose to form a council of six respected companions to deliberate and choose the next caliph. These six individuals—Ali ibn Abi Talib, Uthman ibn Affan, Abdur-Rahman ibn Awf, Sa'd ibn Abi Waqqas, Zubair ibn al-Awwam, and Talha ibn Ubaydullah—were all men of wisdom, experience, and moral integrity.

By appointing this council, Omar ensured that the next leader would be chosen through a process of consultation and consensus, rather than through a singular decision. This demonstrated his deep respect for the collective wisdom of his companions and his understanding that leadership, especially of the growing Muslim community, required legitimacy that could only come from broad agreement among trusted figures. Omar's appointment of the council was an act of humility, as it showed his willingness to share authority and trust in the judgment of others.

The council was given the responsibility of deliberating among themselves and selecting the next caliph within a specified period. They were encouraged to discuss openly and honestly, weighing the strengths and qualities of potential candidates. Omar's decision to entrust this process to his companions also ensured that the leadership transition would be smooth and that the next caliph would have the support of key figures within the Muslim community. Ultimately, the council selected Uthman ibn Affan as the next caliph, a decision that was accepted by the wider community and contributed to the continuity and stability of leadership after Omar's passing.

Omar's reliance on Shura did not end with the appointment of the council. Throughout his reign, he made it a point to consult with people from various walks of life, including scholars, military commanders, and ordinary citizens. He often sought advice on matters of law, governance, and military campaigns, knowing that different perspectives could help him make more informed decisions. This practice of consultation was not only a reflection of his leadership style but also a fulfillment of the Islamic principle that rulers should seek the counsel of others in matters of importance.

One key example of this is seen in Omar's military decisions during the rapid expansion of the Islamic empire. Before launching military campaigns, Omar would consult with his commanders and advisors to discuss strategy, logistics, and the potential impact of the campaigns on both the Muslim community and the regions being targeted. His willingness to listen to others ensured that his decisions were well-considered and based on a broad understanding of the situation. This practice of Shura helped him avoid rash decisions and led to a more successful and strategic expansion of the empire.

Omar's commitment to consultation was also evident in his governance of internal affairs. For example, he sought the advice of companions and scholars on issues related to the welfare of the people, the fair distribution of resources, and the administration of justice. By involving others in these decisions, Omar ensured that the voices of the community were heard and that policies were shaped by a diversity of perspectives. His practice of Shura created a sense of inclusiveness and accountability, as those involved in the decision-making process felt responsible for the outcomes.

In conclusion, Omar's practice of Shura was a defining characteristic of his leadership, reflecting his belief in the value of collective wisdom. By consulting with others and involving trusted individuals in decision-making, he ensured that his governance was fair, inclusive, and rooted in justice. His appointment of a council to choose the next caliph was a particularly powerful example of his commitment to consultation, demonstrating his trust in the wisdom of others and his humility as a leader. For modern leaders, Omar's use of Shura offers a timeless lesson: leadership is most effective when it is based on collaboration, shared responsibility, and the recognition that no single person has all the answers.

The Power of Collective Wisdom in Decision-Making

IN LEADERSHIP, THE ability to make sound decisions is essential, but no leader—no matter how experienced or knowledgeable—can possess all the answers. The value of collective wisdom lies in the idea that the best decisions are often made not by a single individual but through the collaboration and input of diverse perspectives. Omar ibn al-Khattab (may Allah be pleased with him) understood this deeply and demonstrated the importance of collective wisdom throughout his leadership by consistently consulting with others before making significant decisions. His practice of Shura, or consultation, emphasized the strength that comes from seeking advice, weighing different viewpoints, and ultimately making informed choices based on a broad understanding of the issue at hand.

Collective decision-making allows leaders to **benefit from diverse expertise and perspectives**. When leaders involve others in the decision-making process, they are able to draw from the knowledge, experiences, and insights of people with different backgrounds and areas of expertise. This diversity of thought leads to more comprehensive solutions, as it allows leaders to consider various angles and potential outcomes that they may not have been aware of on their own. For example, during his reign, Omar regularly sought the counsel of scholars, military commanders, and community leaders, recognizing that their specialized knowledge could help him make more informed and balanced decisions. Modern leaders, similarly, can benefit from the collective wisdom of their teams, advisors, and stakeholders by encouraging open dialogue and collaboration.

One of the key advantages of collective wisdom is that it helps to **minimize bias and prevent errors in judgment**. When decisions are made in isolation, they are more likely to be influenced by personal biases, blind spots, or incomplete information. By consulting others, leaders can challenge their assumptions, uncover new perspectives, and ensure that their decisions are based on a fuller understanding of the issue. Omar's use of Shura helped him avoid rash or impulsive decisions, as he would seek multiple viewpoints before coming to a conclusion. This process of consultation allowed him to make decisions that were not only well-rounded but also supported by a broad consensus, which helped to ensure their success and acceptance.

Another important lesson from Omar's leadership is that **collective decision-making fosters a sense of shared responsibility and ownership**. When people are involved in the decision-making process, they are more likely to support and commit to the outcome, as they feel that their voices have been heard and their contributions valued. This was evident in Omar's appointment of a council to choose the next caliph. By entrusting this important decision to a group of respected companions, Omar ensured that the transition of leadership would be accepted by the community and that the next caliph would have the legitimacy needed to govern effectively. For modern leaders, involving others in decisions not only strengthens the quality of those decisions but also builds unity and cooperation, as people feel invested in the success of the outcome.

Collective wisdom also encourages **innovation and creativity**, as it brings together diverse ideas and approaches. Leaders who actively seek input from a range of voices are more likely to discover innovative solutions to complex problems. By encouraging open dialogue and fostering an environment where people feel comfortable sharing their thoughts, leaders can tap into the collective creativity of their teams or communities. Omar's practice of Shura ensured that decisions were not limited to one person's vision but were shaped by the collective insights of the community, leading to more dynamic and effective governance. Modern leaders who embrace this approach are likely to find that collective decision-making leads to more innovative and adaptable solutions in today's rapidly changing world.

Finally, the use of collective wisdom helps leaders **build trust and credibility**. Leaders who consult others and make decisions transparently demonstrate humility and respect for the perspectives of those they serve. This approach builds trust, as people see that the leader is not acting out of self-interest or a desire for control but is genuinely seeking the best solution for the greater good. Omar's reliance on Shura earned him the respect and loyalty of the people, as they knew he was a leader who valued their input and acted in their best interests. Modern leaders can build similar trust by practicing consultation and ensuring that their decisions reflect the needs and concerns of the broader community or organization.

In conclusion, the value of collective wisdom in decision-making is clear. By involving others in the process, leaders can benefit from diverse perspectives, minimize bias, foster ownership and responsibility, encourage innovation, and build trust. Omar ibn al-Khattab's leadership is a powerful example of how consultation and collaboration lead to more effective and ethical governance. For modern leaders, embracing collective wisdom not only strengthens the quality of decisions but also creates a more inclusive and cooperative environment where everyone feels empowered to contribute to the success of the organization or society.

Fostering Collaboration and Open Dialogue in Modern Leadership

CREATING A CULTURE of collaboration and open dialogue is essential for effective leadership in today's dynamic world. Modern leaders must recognize that the best decisions and strategies are often born from the collective input of diverse teams and stakeholders. By promoting an environment where everyone feels encouraged to contribute their ideas and perspectives, leaders can tap into the full potential of their organizations or communities, resulting in better decision-making, stronger relationships, and more innovative solutions. Omar ibn al-Khattab's (may Allah be pleased with him) use of Shura serves as a powerful model for how leaders can foster such a culture. To apply these principles in today's context, leaders must implement practical steps to encourage collaboration and maintain open communication.

The first step in building a culture of collaboration is to **create formal structures for consultation and feedback**. Leaders can establish advisory boards, councils, or committees composed of individuals with diverse expertise and backgrounds. These bodies should have clearly defined roles and regular opportunities to provide input on major decisions. For example, in a business context, leaders might form cross-functional teams that bring together representatives from different departments to discuss strategy or solve specific challenges. In government or community settings, leaders can create citizen advisory councils or stakeholder groups to ensure that all perspectives are considered in the policymaking process. By institutionalizing consultation, leaders signal that collaboration is not only valued but is a fundamental part of how decisions are made.

Another important aspect of fostering collaboration is to **encourage diversity of thought**. Leaders must actively seek out and include voices from different backgrounds, experiences, and perspectives. This diversity can help prevent groupthink, where everyone agrees without fully exploring alternative viewpoints, and lead to more creative and innovative solutions. Omar's practice of seeking counsel from a wide range of people, including scholars, military leaders, and ordinary citizens, showed the value of hearing from different perspectives. Modern leaders can apply this by ensuring that their teams or advisory groups are diverse in terms of gender, ethnicity, expertise, and experience. A diverse group brings fresh ideas and new approaches to the table, enriching the decision-making process.

Promoting transparency and open communication is another key to building a collaborative culture. Leaders should be clear about their goals, the rationale behind decisions, and the outcomes they expect. This transparency helps create an environment where people feel empowered to contribute, knowing that their input will be considered and valued. Leaders can facilitate this by holding regular meetings where updates are provided, and open discussions are encouraged. In addition to formal meetings, leaders can create channels for ongoing communication, such as suggestion boxes, online platforms, or town hall-style forums where employees or community members can share their ideas and concerns. By making communication open and accessible, leaders show that they value input from all levels of the organization or society.

Creating a safe and respectful environment is also crucial for encouraging open dialogue. Leaders must ensure that people feel comfortable sharing their ideas and concerns without fear of criticism or retaliation. Omar ibn al-Khattab was known for his humility and willingness to listen to even the most critical voices, demonstrating that a leader must be open to feedback from all sides. Modern leaders can create this sense of safety by fostering a culture of respect, where all contributions are valued, and no one is penalized for expressing a different opinion. Leaders can model this behavior by actively listening, asking questions, and acknowledging the contributions of others, regardless of their rank or status.

Empowering individuals to take ownership of decisions and projects is another way to promote collaboration. When people are given the authority to make decisions and take responsibility for the outcomes, they become more invested in the success of the initiative. Leaders can delegate decision-making authority to teams or individuals who are closest to the issue, allowing them to take the lead on specific projects or challenges. This not only encourages collaboration but also fosters a sense of accountability and ownership. For example, a business leader might empower a team to develop a new product line, giving them the freedom to make key decisions while providing guidance and support as needed. This level of autonomy encourages creativity and collaboration, as team members work together to achieve a common goal.

Leaders should also make an effort to **recognize and reward collaboration**. When people see that their efforts to work together are appreciated, they are more likely to continue fostering a collaborative environment. Leaders can publicly acknowledge individuals or teams who have successfully worked together to solve a problem or achieve a goal. This recognition can take many forms, from verbal praise in meetings to formal awards or incentives. By celebrating collaborative efforts, leaders reinforce the idea that working together is not only valued but is an essential part of the organization's success.

Lastly, leaders must be **open to feedback and willing to adapt**. Collaboration is not a one-way street, and leaders must be prepared to listen to the input they receive and make adjustments when necessary. Omar's willingness to change his decisions based on the counsel of others is a powerful example of how leaders can benefit from being flexible and responsive to new information. Modern leaders can apply this by being open to criticism, regularly soliciting feedback, and making adjustments to strategies or policies when needed. This openness not only strengthens decision-making but also builds trust and respect within the organization or community.

In conclusion, fostering a culture of collaboration and open dialogue requires intentional actions from modern leaders. By creating formal structures for consultation, encouraging diversity of thought, promoting transparency, ensuring a safe environment for dialogue, empowering individuals, recognizing collaborative efforts, and being open to feedback, leaders can build an environment where collective wisdom thrives. Omar ibn al-Khattab's leadership shows the immense value of consultation and collaboration, and by applying these principles, modern leaders can strengthen their organizations and lead more effectively in today's complex world.

Chapter 6: Self-Discipline and Piety: The Foundation of Ethical Leadership

Omar ibn al-Khattab (may Allah be pleased with him) was not only a powerful political and military leader but also a man of profound personal devotion and self-discipline. His leadership was deeply rooted in his spiritual life and his commitment to living according to the principles of Islam. Through his regular prayers, fasting, acts of charity, and strict adherence to moral values, Omar exemplified how self-discipline serves as the foundation of ethical leadership. His life demonstrates that a leader's strength comes not from authority alone, but from their ability to remain grounded in their beliefs and maintain integrity in every aspect of their leadership.

Omar's spiritual discipline was evident in his daily life. Despite his immense responsibilities as caliph, he remained committed to his regular prayers, fasting during Ramadan, and performing other acts of worship. His devotion to prayer, both obligatory and voluntary, was unwavering, reflecting his belief that a leader must maintain a close connection with Allah to guide their actions. Prayer was not just a religious duty for Omar; it was a source of strength and clarity that helped him remain focused on his responsibilities. He believed that a leader must always turn to Allah for guidance, especially when faced with difficult decisions or challenges.

Fasting was another important aspect of Omar's self-discipline. Even during times of hardship, such as droughts or famine, Omar chose to fast alongside his people, sharing in their struggles. His self-discipline extended beyond physical restraint—his fasting symbolized his deep empathy for the suffering of others and his willingness to lead by example. Omar's personal sacrifices, including going without food, demonstrated his commitment to justice and fairness. He refused to indulge in luxuries or privileges that were not available to the people he governed, showing that a leader must remain connected to the needs and experiences of the community.

Charity was also central to Omar's spiritual life. He was known for his generosity, regularly giving to the poor and ensuring that the most vulnerable in society were cared for. His acts of charity were not limited to financial contributions; he would often personally distribute food and resources to those in need. This hands-on approach reflected his belief that leadership is about serving others and that self-discipline involves not only refraining from excess but also giving back to the community. For Omar, charity was a way to live out the values of justice and compassion that defined his leadership.

For modern leaders, Omar's life provides a powerful lesson in the importance of self-discipline and adherence to core values. In a world where leaders are often tempted by power, wealth, and influence, maintaining personal discipline is essential for ethical leadership. Self-discipline allows leaders to stay true to their principles, resist the distractions and temptations of power, and remain focused on their responsibilities to the people they serve. Leaders who practice self-discipline set an example for others, demonstrating that true leadership comes from within and is based on integrity, empathy, and a commitment to justice.

Developing self-discipline as a leader requires a conscious effort to prioritize personal values and moral principles over short-term gains or personal desires. One way modern leaders can cultivate self-discipline is by **establishing regular routines for personal reflection and growth**. Just as Omar dedicated time to prayer and worship, modern leaders can benefit from regular periods of reflection, meditation, or spiritual practice. This helps leaders stay connected to their core values and maintain a sense of purpose in their work. Reflection also allows leaders to assess their actions and decisions, ensuring that they remain aligned with their ethical standards.

Another way to build self-discipline is through **personal accountability**. Leaders must hold themselves to the same high standards they expect from others, and this requires constant self-monitoring. Omar's refusal to indulge in luxuries or privileges as caliph serves as a reminder that leaders must be willing to make personal sacrifices for the greater good. Modern leaders can apply this by setting clear boundaries around their own behavior and resisting the temptations of power or self-interest. This might involve avoiding conflicts of interest, ensuring transparency in financial dealings, or abstaining from privileges that could create a divide between the leader and the people they serve.

Leading by example is another essential component of self-discipline. Omar's actions reflected his commitment to justice, fairness, and humility, and he consistently modeled these values in his leadership. Modern leaders can develop self-discipline by consistently demonstrating ethical behavior in all aspects of their leadership. Whether it's treating employees with respect, making decisions that prioritize the well-being of the community, or remaining humble in the face of success, leading by example ensures that a leader's actions align with their values. This not only reinforces the leader's integrity but also inspires others to act with similar discipline and commitment.

In addition to personal reflection and accountability, leaders can strengthen their self-discipline through **service to others**. Omar's acts of charity and his willingness to share in the struggles of his people show that self-discipline is not just about personal restraint but about using one's resources and influence to benefit others. Modern leaders can follow this example by engaging in service-oriented leadership, where the focus is on meeting the needs of the people and contributing to the greater good. This might involve participating in community initiatives, supporting social justice causes, or ensuring that policies and decisions benefit the most vulnerable members of society.

In conclusion, self-discipline and piety were central to Omar ibn al-Khattab's leadership, guiding his actions and ensuring that his rule was marked by justice, fairness, and compassion. For modern leaders, self-discipline is a key component of ethical leadership, allowing them to remain grounded in their values and lead with integrity. By prioritizing personal reflection, accountability, leading by example, and focusing on service to others, leaders can develop the self-discipline needed to guide their decisions and actions. Omar's life demonstrates that true leadership is not just about power or authority—it is about maintaining inner strength, humility, and a commitment to serving others in the pursuit of justice.

Omar's Personal Devotion: A Life Rooted in Faith and Discipline

OMAR IBN AL-KHATTAB (may Allah be pleased with him) was known for his deep sense of personal devotion, which guided every aspect of his life and leadership. His commitment to prayer, fasting, and charity was not just a reflection of his faith but also the foundation of his moral integrity and discipline as a leader. Omar's spiritual life was characterized by an unwavering dedication to living according to the principles of Islam, and this devotion shaped his actions as caliph. His ability to balance the immense responsibilities of leadership with his personal acts of worship and charity serves as a powerful example of how faith and discipline can strengthen one's ability to lead with justice and compassion.

Prayer was central to Omar's daily life. Despite being the leader of a vast and rapidly expanding empire, he never allowed his political or military duties to interfere with his spiritual obligations. Omar was diligent in performing the five daily prayers and made time for additional voluntary prayers (nawafil), which further deepened his connection with Allah. For Omar, prayer was not just a ritual—it was a source of strength, guidance, and clarity. It helped him remain grounded in his faith and provided him with the spiritual resilience needed to lead with wisdom and justice. His commitment to prayer also served as an example to those around him, reinforcing the importance of maintaining one's relationship with Allah, regardless of worldly responsibilities.

Fasting was another pillar of Omar's personal devotion. Like all Muslims, Omar fasted during the month of Ramadan, but his commitment to fasting went beyond the obligatory fasts. During times of hardship, such as famine or drought, Omar would fast in solidarity with the people, refusing to eat more than what the poorest among them had access to. His famous practice of eating only bread and oil during such times demonstrated his deep empathy for the struggles of the people and his desire to share in their suffering. Omar believed that a leader should never indulge in comforts that the common people could not enjoy, and his fasting was a way of holding himself accountable to that principle. His discipline in fasting showed that self-restraint and empathy were key elements of his leadership, and that a true leader must be willing to sacrifice personal comfort for the greater good.

Charity, or **sadaqah**, was another important aspect of Omar's personal devotion. He was known for his generosity and his commitment to ensuring that the most vulnerable members of society were cared for. Omar regularly gave from his own wealth to support the poor, the widowed, and the orphaned, seeing this as both a religious duty and a moral responsibility. However, his acts of charity were not limited to financial contributions. Omar would often personally distribute food and resources to those in need, ensuring that they received not only material support but also the dignity of being acknowledged by their leader. This hands-on approach to charity reflected Omar's belief that leadership is about service and that true piety involves actively working to alleviate the suffering of others.

One of the most well-known stories of Omar's personal charity involves a night when he overheard a woman struggling to provide food for her children. Without revealing his identity, Omar went to the public treasury, collected supplies, and delivered them to the woman's home himself. When his companion offered to carry the burden for him, Omar declined, stating, "Will you carry my burden on the Day of Judgment?" This story encapsulates Omar's deep sense of personal responsibility and his understanding that leadership required direct involvement in the welfare of the people. His acts of charity were not motivated by a desire for recognition but by his genuine commitment to justice and compassion.

Omar's spiritual life, marked by prayer, fasting, and charity, was not separate from his leadership—it was the foundation of it. His devotion to Allah guided his decisions as a leader and gave him the moral strength to lead with fairness, humility, and empathy. Omar's discipline in fulfilling his religious duties also set an example for the Muslim community, showing that success in this world must never come at the expense of one's relationship with Allah. His balance of faith and leadership demonstrates that the most effective leaders are those who lead not just with their minds but with their hearts, grounded in spiritual discipline and a sense of responsibility to the people they serve.

In conclusion, Omar ibn al-Khattab's personal devotion was a defining feature of his leadership. His commitment to prayer, fasting, and charity was a testament to his deep faith and his belief that leadership must be rooted in moral integrity and service to others. Through his spiritual discipline, Omar was able to lead with compassion, fairness, and a clear sense of purpose, always striving to fulfill his duties to Allah and to the people he governed. His life serves as a powerful reminder that true leadership is not about power or authority but about living according to one's principles and using that strength to benefit others.

The Role of Self-Discipline in Ethical Leadership

SELF-DISCIPLINE IS a fundamental trait that distinguishes ethical leaders from those who are merely in positions of authority. For modern leaders, the ability to remain steadfast in their principles, even when faced with challenges, temptations, or pressures, is essential to maintaining integrity and building trust. Omar ibn al-Khattab (may Allah be pleased with him) exemplified this through his leadership, where his self-discipline and adherence to core Islamic values shaped his governance and inspired those around him. His life offers a timeless lesson on how self-discipline not only strengthens leadership but also serves as a guide for making just and ethical decisions.

Self-discipline begins with a commitment to **core values**, which act as a moral compass for leaders. These values—whether rooted in personal beliefs, religious teachings, or ethical frameworks—provide the foundation for all decisions and actions. For Omar, his core values were shaped by his deep commitment to Islam and its principles of justice, fairness, and compassion. His self-discipline in prayer, fasting, and charity was a reflection of these values, showing that his personal life was aligned with the same standards he set for his public leadership. Modern leaders can learn from this by ensuring that their actions, both in private and in public, are consistently aligned with their core values, creating a foundation of trust and authenticity.

In leadership, **self-discipline is essential for maintaining focus and consistency**. Leaders are often pulled in many directions, facing conflicting interests, short-term gains, or external pressures. Without self-discipline, it is easy to stray from one's ethical path or compromise values for convenience. Omar's leadership demonstrated that self-discipline allows leaders to stay committed to their long-term goals and maintain ethical standards, even when faced with adversity. His refusal to indulge in luxuries while others suffered, his dedication to fasting during times of hardship, and his personal sacrifices all highlighted his ability to stay true to his values regardless of external circumstances. Modern leaders can apply this lesson by developing the self-discipline needed to prioritize the greater good over immediate, self-serving benefits.

A leader's self-discipline also **sets a powerful example** for those they lead. When leaders demonstrate consistency in their ethical behavior, they inspire others to follow suit. People are more likely to respect and trust a leader who leads by example, practicing the values they preach. Omar's life is a clear testament to this, as his humility, fairness, and personal restraint earned him the respect of those around him, both Muslim and non-Muslim alike. Modern leaders, by embodying self-discipline, encourage a culture of accountability and ethical behavior throughout their organizations or communities. This example helps create an environment where integrity is valued, and unethical behavior is less likely to be tolerated.

Furthermore, **self-discipline is crucial for resisting the corrupting influence of power**. Power can be intoxicating, and without self-discipline, leaders may find themselves making decisions based on personal gain rather than the welfare of the people they serve. Omar's leadership was marked by his ability to resist the temptations of power and remain humble despite his authority. He held himself to the same standards as everyone else, refusing any special privileges or indulgences. His actions remind modern leaders that power is a responsibility, not a right, and that maintaining self-discipline is key to avoiding the arrogance or corruption that often comes with authority.

Leaders who adhere to their core values are also better equipped to **make difficult, but necessary, ethical decisions**. In many situations, leaders are required to make tough choices that may not always be popular or easy but are necessary for justice and fairness. Omar's self-discipline allowed him to make decisions that were in the best interest of the people, even when they were personally difficult. For example, his commitment to justice led him to remove governors or officials who abused their power, regardless of their status or relationship to him. Modern leaders can learn from this by recognizing that self-discipline helps them stay focused on their ethical responsibilities, allowing them to make decisions that are fair, just, and in line with their core values, even in the face of opposition.

In conclusion, self-discipline is a cornerstone of ethical leadership. It ensures that leaders remain committed to their core values, act consistently, and make decisions based on principles rather than expediency. Omar ibn al-Khattab's life demonstrates how self-discipline can guide leaders to maintain integrity, resist the temptations of power, and inspire others to uphold high ethical standards. For modern leaders, cultivating self-discipline is essential for building trust, ensuring fairness, and leading with purpose and integrity.

Developing Self-Discipline: Leading by Example

SELF-DISCIPLINE IS not an inherent trait but a skill that can be developed over time with conscious effort and commitment. For leaders, cultivating self-discipline is essential for maintaining ethical standards, making sound decisions, and setting a positive example for others to follow. Leaders who practice self-discipline demonstrate their commitment to their core values and inspire trust and respect from those they lead. Omar ibn al-Khattab (may Allah be pleased with him) exemplified this through his consistent actions of self-restraint, humility, and service to others. Modern leaders can learn from his example by adopting practical steps to develop self-discipline and lead with integrity.

The first step in developing self-discipline is to **establish clear personal and professional values**. Leaders need to be firmly grounded in the principles they want to uphold, whether these are based on ethical, moral, or spiritual beliefs. By identifying and committing to these values, leaders create a solid foundation for their actions and decisions. Omar's adherence to justice, fairness, and humility in his leadership was a direct result of his commitment to the core teachings of Islam. Modern leaders should take time to reflect on their own guiding principles, ensuring that these values align with their vision for leadership and governance. Once these values are established, leaders must consistently refer back to them when making decisions, allowing their values to guide their actions.

To cultivate self-discipline, leaders should also **create structured routines** that reinforce their values. Just as Omar made time for regular prayer, fasting, and acts of charity, modern leaders can benefit from routines that promote personal growth and self-discipline. This could involve setting aside time each day for reflection, meditation, or spiritual practices, which help leaders stay connected to their core values and develop a sense of inner strength. Additionally, leaders can establish routines that promote accountability and continuous improvement, such as setting personal goals, tracking progress, and evaluating their actions against their ethical standards.

Setting clear boundaries and practicing restraint is another critical aspect of self-discipline. Leaders are often faced with opportunities to indulge in personal gain, comfort, or privilege, but true leadership requires the ability to resist these temptations for the greater good. Omar's decision to fast during times of hardship, even when food was available to him, exemplifies his ability to practice self-restraint. Modern leaders can apply this principle by avoiding excessive luxuries, refusing privileges that separate them from those they serve, and making personal sacrifices when necessary. By setting boundaries around their behavior, leaders show that they are committed to serving the people rather than serving themselves.

Leaders can also develop self-discipline by **holding themselves accountable** for their actions. This involves regularly reflecting on decisions and behaviors, identifying areas for improvement, and being honest about mistakes. Omar was known for his humility and willingness to admit when he was wrong, often seeking forgiveness from the people and making amends. Modern leaders should cultivate the same level of accountability by creating feedback mechanisms, seeking input from trusted advisors, and regularly assessing their performance against their ethical standards. Accountability not only strengthens self-discipline but also reinforces transparency and trust within the organization or community.

Leading by example is perhaps the most powerful way for leaders to demonstrate self-discipline. When leaders consistently practice what they preach, they set a standard for others to follow. Omar's leadership was defined by his ability to lead by example, whether through his personal humility, his dedication to prayer and fasting, or his commitment to justice. Modern leaders can apply this by ensuring that their actions align with their words, particularly when it comes to ethical standards. If a leader expects honesty, fairness, and hard work from their team, they must embody these qualities in their own behavior. By modeling self-discipline, leaders inspire those around them to adopt the same level of integrity and commitment.

Another important practice is to **develop resilience and patience**. Self-discipline often requires enduring challenges, setbacks, or pressures without losing sight of one's values. Omar's life as caliph was filled with difficulties, yet his ability to remain steadfast in his beliefs allowed him to navigate complex issues with wisdom and clarity. Modern leaders can build resilience by focusing on long-term goals, remaining patient during challenging times, and using adversity as an opportunity for growth. Cultivating resilience helps leaders stay disciplined even in the face of obstacles, ensuring that they continue to lead with integrity.

Finally, leaders must **foster a culture of discipline within their teams or organizations**. Self-discipline is not just an individual trait; it can be cultivated throughout an organization by setting clear expectations, establishing consistent standards, and encouraging ethical behavior at all levels. Leaders can create policies and practices that reward discipline and integrity, ensuring that these values are embedded in the organizational culture. By leading with discipline and fostering the same in others, leaders create an environment where ethical behavior becomes the norm, not the exception.

In conclusion, developing self-discipline is essential for effective and ethical leadership. By establishing clear values, creating structured routines, practicing restraint, holding themselves accountable, leading by example, building resilience, and fostering a culture of discipline, leaders can cultivate the self-discipline needed to guide their decisions and actions. Omar ibn al-Khattab's life serves as a powerful model of how self-discipline can shape ethical leadership, and modern leaders can apply these principles to lead with integrity and inspire others to do the same.

Part III: Courage, Empathy, and Visionary Leadership: The Pillars of Lasting Leadership

Leadership requires more than authority or control; it demands courage to make difficult decisions, empathy to understand the needs of the people, and a vision that goes beyond immediate concerns. Omar ibn al-Khattab (may Allah be pleased with him) embodied these traits, making bold decisions during times of expansion, showing deep compassion for the vulnerable, and laying the foundation for systems that would benefit generations to come. His leadership style was not only about addressing the challenges of his time but also about creating lasting change through foresight, resilience, and care for others.

Courage was central to Omar's leadership, as he navigated the challenges of rapidly expanding the Islamic empire and maintaining justice within it. His determination to uphold justice, even when it was difficult or unpopular, set him apart as a leader who was unafraid to make tough decisions for the greater good. Omar understood that leadership sometimes requires taking bold, decisive actions that may not always be well-received in the moment but are necessary for long-term success.

Empathy was another cornerstone of Omar's governance. His deep concern for the poor, orphans, and widows drove him to establish welfare systems that ensured the most vulnerable members of society were cared for. Omar's ability to put himself in the shoes of the people he governed allowed him to lead with compassion, making decisions that were not just about power or expansion but about improving the lives of those under his rule. His acts of charity and personal involvement in helping those in need reflected his belief that leadership is ultimately about service.

Visionary leadership is what allowed Omar to build enduring systems that went beyond his lifetime. His administrative reforms, military organization, and introduction of the Islamic calendar were all part of his long-term strategy to ensure that the Muslim community would thrive for generations to come. Omar's ability to think beyond the immediate challenges of his time and create structures that would sustain the community well into the future is a powerful example of what true visionary leadership entails.

In this part of the book, we will explore these three critical aspects of leadership—courage, empathy, and visionary thinking—and how they shaped Omar's rule. Each chapter will examine how modern leaders can apply these principles to tackle difficult decisions, build compassionate governance, and create long-term strategies that lead to lasting success. By embracing these pillars of leadership, today's leaders can make a meaningful impact on their communities and leave a legacy of justice, compassion, and progress.

Chapter 7: Courage and Determination: The Backbone of Leadership

Omar ibn al-Khattab (may Allah be pleased with him) was known for his remarkable courage and unwavering determination, qualities that were critical during his time as caliph of the rapidly expanding Islamic empire. Courage was not just a personal trait for Omar—it was an essential part of his leadership, guiding him through moments of great challenge and controversy. His bold decisions, made during times of war, crisis, and societal change, shaped the future of the Islamic state and solidified his reputation as a leader who was unafraid to do what was right, even when it was difficult. For Omar, courage meant standing firm in the face of adversity and making decisions based on principles rather than fear or popularity.

One of the most notable examples of Omar's courage was during the rapid expansion of the Islamic empire. After the death of the Prophet Muhammad (peace be upon him) and the leadership of the first caliph, Abu Bakr, Omar took charge of an empire that was not only growing geographically but also facing internal and external threats. The decision to continue expanding the empire into the Byzantine and Sassanian territories required tremendous courage, as it involved leading the Muslim community into uncertain and dangerous conflicts. Omar's determination to ensure the success of these campaigns, despite the risks, demonstrated his ability to stay focused on long-term goals, while also making difficult decisions that had far-reaching consequences.

In addition to his military leadership, Omar displayed immense courage in his efforts to uphold justice within his empire. He was unafraid to confront powerful figures, including governors and military commanders, when they acted unjustly. One famous instance of his courage involved his removal of the governor of Egypt, Amr ibn al-As, after complaints of unjust treatment were brought to Omar's attention. Despite Amr's influence and military achievements, Omar stood firm in his commitment to justice and fairness, showing that no one, no matter their status, was above the law. This bold decision reinforced his belief that courage in leadership is not only about military strength but also about standing up for what is right, even when it is unpopular.

For modern leaders, the lesson from Omar's leadership is clear: courage is essential for making difficult and sometimes controversial decisions. Leadership often requires stepping into the unknown, making choices that may not please everyone, and standing firm in the face of resistance. Whether it's addressing systemic injustices, implementing reforms that challenge the status quo, or leading through crises, leaders must have the courage to take bold actions when necessary. Without courage, leaders may succumb to fear, indecision, or the pressures of public opinion, leading to stagnation or failure to address critical issues.

To cultivate courage and resilience, modern leaders can start by **building a strong sense of purpose**. Omar's courage came from his deep commitment to justice and the values of Islam, which gave him the strength to make bold decisions, even in the face of opposition. Modern leaders can benefit from reflecting on their core values and the larger mission they serve. When leaders are clear about their purpose, they are more likely to find the courage to make difficult decisions, knowing that they are guided by principles rather than personal gain or fear.

Another strategy for developing courage is to **embrace challenges and uncertainty**. Leaders like Omar did not shy away from challenges—they faced them head-on. By developing a mindset that sees challenges as opportunities for growth and progress, leaders can build resilience and the confidence needed to tackle difficult situations. This involves accepting that uncertainty and risk are inherent parts of leadership and that courage comes from navigating these challenges with determination and a clear vision for the future.

Leaders can also cultivate courage by **seeking counsel and trusting in collective wisdom**. While courage often involves making tough decisions, it does not mean acting in isolation. Omar was known for consulting with his companions and advisors before making important decisions, ensuring that his actions were informed by diverse perspectives. Modern leaders can build their courage by surrounding themselves with trusted advisors who provide support, insight, and alternative viewpoints. By relying on collective wisdom, leaders can feel more confident in their decisions, knowing that they have considered all angles and are acting in the best interest of the people.

Lastly, **courage can be developed through experience and reflection**. Every difficult decision a leader makes is an opportunity to build resilience and strength for future challenges. Omar's courage was not born overnight—it was cultivated through years of leadership experience, facing both successes and setbacks. Modern leaders can take a similar approach by reflecting on their past experiences, learning from their mistakes, and using those lessons to strengthen their resolve for the future. Each decision, no matter how small, contributes to the development of courage and the ability to make even bolder decisions as challenges arise.

In conclusion, courage and determination are vital traits for leaders who seek to make a lasting impact. Omar ibn al-Khattab's leadership provides a powerful example of how bold decisions, driven by principles, can shape the course of history. For modern leaders, cultivating courage involves building a strong sense of purpose, embracing challenges, seeking counsel, and reflecting on experiences to develop resilience. Courage in leadership is not about avoiding fear but facing it with confidence, knowing that difficult decisions, when guided by ethical principles, lead to progress and lasting success.

Omar's Bold Decisions: Courage in the Face of Uncertainty

OMAR IBN AL-KHATTAB (may Allah be pleased with him) is remembered as one of the most courageous leaders in Islamic history, known for his decisive actions and bold leadership during some of the most challenging periods of the early Islamic empire. His tenure as the second caliph was marked by rapid territorial expansion, internal reforms, and a steadfast commitment to justice, all of which required immense courage and determination. These moments of bold decision-making not only expanded the Islamic empire but also established a legacy of justice and strength that endures to this day.

One of the most significant examples of Omar's courage was his leadership during the **rapid expansion of the Islamic empire**. Upon assuming the caliphate, Omar inherited a state that was already growing beyond the Arabian Peninsula, but his leadership marked a turning point in its further expansion into the Byzantine and Sassanian empires. This expansion was fraught with challenges, including fierce resistance from established powers and internal questions about the risks of overextension. Nevertheless, Omar made the bold decision to press forward, leading military campaigns into territories such as Syria, Iraq, Egypt, and Persia. These conquests were not merely about acquiring land but also about spreading the message of Islam and establishing justice in newly acquired regions.

Omar's courage was particularly evident during the **Battle of Yarmouk** in 636 CE, a decisive battle against the Byzantine Empire.

Despite being vastly outnumbered, Omar's decision to proceed with the battle reflected his unshakable belief in the strength of the Muslim army and his faith in Allah's guidance. The victory at Yarmouk solidified Muslim control over the Levant and became a turning point in the expansion of the Islamic state. Omar's bold decision to continue fighting in the face of overwhelming odds demonstrated his willingness to take calculated risks for the sake of long-term success.

Another key moment that showcased Omar's courage was his **decision to confront and defeat the Sassanian Empire**. The Sassanian Empire was one of the most powerful forces in the world at the time, and the decision to engage in a series of military campaigns against them was not without significant risk. Omar knew that challenging such a formidable empire would require both military strategy and immense courage. One of the most notable battles was the **Battle of al-Qadisiyyah** in 636 CE, where the Muslim forces, under the leadership of Sa'd ibn Abi Waqqas, successfully defeated the Sassanian army. This victory led to the conquest of the Sassanian capital, Ctesiphon, and marked the decline of the Sassanian Empire. Omar's decision to pursue this campaign, despite the challenges, reflected his ability to make bold, strategic choices in the face of uncertainty.

Omar's courage was not limited to military conquests. He also made bold decisions in governance, particularly in his **reforms of the Islamic state**. One of the most significant reforms was the creation of the **diwan**, a system of financial administration that organized the distribution of wealth and resources among the Muslim community. This decision was bold because it represented a shift from a more informal system of governance to a structured, bureaucratic model. By establishing the diwan, Omar ensured that the growing wealth of the Islamic empire was distributed fairly, and resources were managed efficiently. This reform required not only administrative foresight but also the courage to implement a system that would reshape how the state functioned.

Omar's courage in leadership was also evident in his **commitment to justice**, even when it involved making difficult decisions against powerful individuals. One example of this was his removal of **Khalid ibn al-Walid**, one of the most successful military commanders in Islamic history, from his position as commander of the army. Despite Khalid's victories on the battlefield, there were concerns about his methods and his increasing influence. Omar, determined to uphold justice and prevent any potential abuse of power, made the difficult decision to relieve Khalid of his command. This bold move demonstrated Omar's courage in placing the principles of justice above personal relationships or military success, showing that no one, not even a revered general, was above accountability.

In conclusion, Omar's bold decisions during the expansion of the Islamic empire, his governance reforms, and his commitment to justice highlight his extraordinary courage as a leader. His willingness to take risks, confront powerful enemies, and make difficult choices, even when they were unpopular, solidified his legacy as a caliph who led with strength and conviction. Omar's courage continues to serve as a model for leaders today, showing that bold decision-making, guided by principles of justice and faith, is essential for achieving lasting success.

The Necessity of Courage in Tackling Difficult and Controversial Decisions

COURAGE IS ONE OF THE most important qualities a leader must possess when faced with difficult or controversial decisions. It is not enough for a leader to simply manage day-to-day affairs; true leadership requires the ability to make bold decisions, particularly when they are unpopular or come with significant risks. Courage allows leaders to act with conviction, guided by their principles and the greater good, rather than being swayed by fear, public opinion, or immediate pressures. Omar ibn al-Khattab (may Allah be pleased with him) demonstrated this kind of leadership throughout his time as caliph, showing that courageous decision-making is essential for creating lasting, positive change.

In leadership, difficult decisions often involve uncertainty, risk, or opposition. Leaders must be willing to confront these challenges directly, rather than avoiding or postponing action out of fear. Courage enables leaders to move forward even when the outcome is unclear or when there is substantial resistance from others. Omar's decision to lead the Muslim community into major battles, such as the Battle of Yarmouk and the campaigns against the Sassanian Empire, are prime examples of this. These were not decisions made lightly, as they involved engaging powerful enemies and risking the safety of his people. Yet, Omar's courage allowed him to see beyond the immediate danger and focus on the long-term benefits of expanding the Islamic state and spreading justice.

Courage is equally important when it comes to confronting internal challenges. Leaders often face situations where they must address misconduct, injustice, or difficult truths within their own organization or community. Omar's courage was evident in his willingness to hold even the most powerful figures accountable, including military leaders like Khalid ibn al-Walid, whom he removed from command despite Khalid's many victories. This decision was controversial and could have led to dissent, yet Omar knew that allowing unchecked power would undermine the values of justice and fairness that he sought to uphold. Modern leaders must also have the courage to confront difficult issues within their organizations, knowing that avoiding them will only lead to greater problems down the road.

One of the key reasons courage is essential in leadership is that it allows leaders to make decisions based on **principles rather than convenience**. Difficult decisions often test a leader's commitment to their values. Without courage, leaders may be tempted to take the easy path, make compromises that go against their core beliefs, or prioritize short-term gains over long-term integrity. Omar's bold decisions in governance, such as his implementation of financial reforms and his removal of unjust governors, showed that he valued justice above all else. His actions were not always popular, but they were driven by his commitment to fairness and accountability. For modern leaders, this lesson is clear: courage allows you to stay true to your principles, even when it means making hard choices.

Courage also plays a critical role in **navigating controversy and opposition.** In leadership, decisions often affect multiple stakeholders, and it's impossible to please everyone. Leaders who lack courage may become paralyzed by fear of criticism, conflict, or backlash. However, courageous leaders understand that controversy is an inevitable part of leadership, and they are willing to take the necessary steps for the greater good, even if it means facing opposition. Omar's leadership in expanding the Islamic empire required facing not only external enemies but also internal debates about the risks and challenges of such expansion. His courage in moving forward, despite these concerns, demonstrates that sometimes the most impactful decisions are the ones that come with the greatest opposition.

Modern leaders can apply this lesson by cultivating the ability to **embrace conflict and uncertainty.** Courage does not mean being reckless or ignoring risks; rather, it means having the confidence to take action when it is needed, even when the outcome is uncertain. Leaders must be prepared to make decisions that may cause discomfort or stir controversy, recognizing that true progress often requires pushing through difficult moments. Whether it is implementing a new policy that challenges the status quo or confronting unethical behavior within an organization, courageous leadership is about taking action in service of a larger goal, even when the path is difficult.

Finally, courage is essential for building **resilience and long-term success.** Leaders who act with courage inspire trust and loyalty from those they lead, as people are more likely to follow a leader who is decisive and unafraid to stand by their convictions. Omar's courageous decisions during his time as caliph not only expanded the Islamic empire but also solidified the trust of the people, who knew that he would always act with their best interests in mind. Modern leaders, too, can build resilience in their organizations by showing that they are willing to make tough decisions for the right reasons, creating a culture of trust, integrity, and strength.

In conclusion, courage is a vital component of leadership when facing difficult and controversial decisions. It allows leaders to act with conviction, uphold their principles, and navigate conflict and opposition with confidence. Omar ibn al-Khattab's leadership provides a powerful example of how courageous decision-making can lead to lasting success and positive change. Modern leaders can learn from his example by cultivating courage in their own leadership, ensuring that they are prepared to tackle difficult issues with integrity and determination, always guided by their values and the greater good.

Cultivating Courage and Resilience in Leadership

COURAGE AND RESILIENCE are essential qualities that enable leaders to navigate challenges, make tough decisions, and inspire those they lead. Developing these traits requires intentional practice and self-awareness. Leadership is not without adversity, and the ability to remain steadfast in the face of uncertainty or opposition is what separates effective leaders from the rest. Just as Omar ibn al-Khattab (may Allah be pleased with him) demonstrated immense courage and resilience in his leadership, modern leaders must actively cultivate these qualities to lead with integrity and strength.

One of the key strategies for cultivating courage in leadership is to **build a strong sense of purpose and values**. Leaders who are grounded in their principles and have a clear vision of their mission are better equipped to make difficult decisions with confidence. Having a strong purpose gives leaders a foundation to rely on when faced with challenges. Omar's courage stemmed from his deep commitment to justice and fairness, which guided his every decision. Modern leaders can similarly develop courage by reflecting on their core values and aligning their actions with those beliefs. When a leader's decisions are rooted in a larger purpose, it becomes easier to stand firm in the face of adversity, knowing that the decisions are made for the right reasons.

Another important strategy is to **embrace calculated risks**. Courage in leadership often involves stepping into the unknown and taking risks that may not guarantee immediate success. Leaders who shy away from risk are more likely to stagnate and miss opportunities for growth and progress. Omar's decision to engage in battles like Yarmouk and the conquest of the Sassanian Empire, despite the risks involved, exemplified his ability to take bold, calculated risks that ultimately strengthened the Islamic empire. Modern leaders can cultivate courage by learning to evaluate risks carefully, weighing the potential rewards against the dangers, and making informed decisions. The key is to embrace risk while remaining vigilant and prepared to adapt when necessary.

Developing emotional resilience is another crucial element in cultivating courage. Leaders must be able to recover from setbacks, criticism, and failure without losing confidence in their abilities. Resilience allows leaders to persevere through difficult times and maintain their composure when faced with challenges. To build resilience, leaders should focus on maintaining a growth mindset—viewing failures as learning opportunities rather than permanent setbacks. Omar's leadership demonstrated resilience in his ability to remain focused on long-term goals despite opposition or challenges along the way. Modern leaders can practice resilience by reflecting on their past experiences, identifying what they have learned from those situations, and applying those lessons to future challenges.

Surrounding oneself with trusted advisors and a support system is another effective strategy for building courage and resilience. Leaders should not feel that they have to make tough decisions alone. Omar regularly consulted his companions and sought their counsel before making important decisions. This practice allowed him to approach challenges with confidence, knowing that he had considered diverse perspectives. Modern leaders can apply this by cultivating a network of trusted advisors who provide honest feedback, guidance, and support. Having a team to rely on not only strengthens decision-making but also helps leaders stay grounded and resilient during difficult times.

Practicing self-discipline and mindfulness is also essential for fostering courage. Leaders who can control their emotions, remain calm under pressure, and act with intention are better equipped to face challenges head-on. Omar's self-discipline in his personal life—through prayer, fasting, and charity—helped him maintain clarity and focus in his leadership. Modern leaders can develop courage by incorporating mindfulness practices such as meditation, reflection, or journaling into their routines. These practices help leaders manage stress, increase emotional intelligence, and approach difficult situations with a clear mind, enabling them to respond with courage rather than react impulsively.

Facing smaller challenges head-on is another way leaders can build their courage over time. Courage, like any skill, is developed through practice. Leaders can start by tackling smaller challenges or making decisions that require a degree of discomfort or risk. As they become more comfortable facing and overcoming these situations, they build the confidence needed to handle larger, more complex challenges. Each courageous decision adds to their resilience and strengthens their ability to lead through adversity. Leaders should seek out opportunities that challenge them, whether it's making a tough call in a meeting, addressing an uncomfortable issue, or stepping into a new leadership role.

Finally, **learning from courageous role models** can provide inspiration and guidance. Studying the lives of leaders like Omar ibn al-Khattab, who demonstrated extraordinary courage and resilience, offers valuable lessons on how to handle difficult situations. Modern leaders can draw inspiration from historical figures or contemporary leaders who have faced adversity and made bold decisions. Learning from their stories can help leaders see how courage can lead to positive outcomes and long-term success, even in the face of overwhelming challenges.

In conclusion, cultivating courage and resilience in leadership is a process that requires a deep connection to one's values, a willingness to take risks, emotional strength, and consistent practice. By building a strong sense of purpose, embracing risks, developing resilience, seeking counsel, practicing mindfulness, and learning from role models, leaders can develop the courage needed to face difficult decisions and inspire those they lead. Omar ibn al-Khattab's leadership serves as a timeless example of how courage, paired with wisdom and determination, can shape the future and leave a lasting impact. Modern leaders who cultivate these qualities will be better equipped to navigate challenges and lead with integrity and strength.

Chapter 8: Empathy and Compassion: A Leader's Duty to the Vulnerable

Omar ibn al-Khattab (may Allah be pleased with him) was not only a bold and decisive leader, but he also embodied deep compassion for the most vulnerable members of society. His leadership was marked by a profound sense of empathy, which guided many of his decisions and policies. Omar recognized that true leadership is not just about expanding territories or enforcing laws but also about caring for those who are most in need—especially the poor, orphans, and widows. His establishment of welfare systems and his personal concern for the well-being of the vulnerable set a powerful example of how leaders must prioritize compassion and empathy in their governance.

Omar's compassion can be seen in his efforts to create and institutionalize social welfare programs that provided direct assistance to the less fortunate. He introduced the concept of a public treasury (*Bayt al-Mal*) that ensured resources were distributed to those in need. This system provided financial support to orphans, widows, and the poor, demonstrating Omar's commitment to a fair and just society. His approach to governance was not merely transactional; it was rooted in the belief that a leader is responsible for the welfare of every member of the community, particularly those who could not support themselves. Omar's compassionate policies ensured that wealth was not concentrated among the elite but was instead shared in a way that uplifted society as a whole.

One of the most notable examples of Omar's empathy was his **concern for orphans and widows.** He understood the vulnerability of these groups and worked tirelessly to protect their rights and dignity. In addition to the financial support provided by the public treasury, Omar personally took it upon himself to ensure that orphans and widows were cared for. It is reported that he would often walk the streets at night to check on the well-being of the people, sometimes even carrying food on his back to deliver to families in need. These acts of personal charity and compassion demonstrated that, for Omar, leadership was not just a position of power—it was a moral responsibility to care for the least fortunate members of society.

For modern leaders, Omar's compassion teaches a critical lesson: empathy is essential in governance. In today's complex world, where economic inequality and social injustice persist, leaders must prioritize the well-being of the vulnerable in their decision-making. Leadership is not simply about economic growth or political stability; it is also about creating systems that support those who are struggling, ensuring that no one is left behind. Empathy enables leaders to understand the lived experiences of the people they serve, allowing them to make more informed and compassionate decisions that address the root causes of social issues.

Empathy in leadership fosters trust, unity, and social harmony. When leaders show genuine concern for the welfare of their people, it creates a sense of solidarity and mutual respect. People are more likely to trust and follow a leader who demonstrates that they care about their needs and struggles. Omar's ability to connect with people on a personal level, through both his policies and his actions, allowed him to build a society where the vulnerable felt supported and protected. Modern leaders can learn from this by actively seeking to understand the challenges faced by marginalized communities and incorporating empathy into their decision-making processes.

To apply this lesson in today's world, modern leaders must focus on **implementing social welfare programs that provide safety nets for the vulnerable.** This involves creating policies that ensure access to essential services like healthcare, education, and housing for low-income individuals and families. Governments and organizations can establish public funds or social programs that offer financial assistance, job training, and social services to help lift people out of poverty and create opportunities for upward mobility. Omar's public treasury model can serve as a blueprint for modern social welfare systems, where resources are allocated to support those who need it most.

Direct engagement with communities is another practical way for leaders to show empathy. Just as Omar walked the streets of Medina at night to check on the well-being of his people, modern leaders should make efforts to engage directly with the communities they serve. This can involve holding town hall meetings, visiting underserved areas, or setting up advisory councils that include representatives from marginalized groups. By listening to the concerns and needs of the people, leaders can gain a deeper understanding of the challenges they face and make decisions that are more responsive to those needs.

Additionally, leaders can demonstrate empathy by **developing policies that address systemic inequalities**. This includes addressing issues such as income inequality, racial and gender disparities, and access to education and healthcare. Modern leaders must recognize that many social problems are deeply rooted in structural inequalities, and addressing these issues requires more than temporary relief. Omar's leadership was marked by his commitment to justice and fairness, and modern leaders can follow his example by working to dismantle systemic barriers that prevent individuals from achieving their full potential.

Finally, leaders can **lead by example** in showing empathy and compassion. Just as Omar personally delivered food to families in need, modern leaders can engage in acts of service that demonstrate their commitment to the well-being of others. This could include volunteering with social organizations, participating in charitable initiatives, or using their platforms to raise awareness about social issues. By taking direct action, leaders show that empathy is not just an abstract concept but a guiding principle that informs their leadership and decision-making.

In conclusion, Omar ibn al-Khattab's leadership exemplifies the power of empathy and compassion in governance. His establishment of welfare systems and his personal concern for the vulnerable demonstrate that true leadership involves caring for the well-being of all members of society, particularly those who are most in need. Modern leaders can apply these principles by prioritizing empathy in their decision-making, implementing social welfare programs, engaging directly with communities, addressing systemic inequalities, and leading by example. In doing so, they can create a more just and compassionate society where every individual is supported and valued.

Omar's Compassion for the Vulnerable: Building a Welfare System for the Poor, Orphans, and Widows

OMAR IBN AL-KHATTAB (may Allah be pleased with him) is widely remembered not only for his leadership and military successes but also for his profound empathy and compassion for the vulnerable members of society. His reign as the second caliph of the Islamic empire was marked by his commitment to ensuring that the poor, orphans, and widows were cared for and that their basic needs were met. Through the establishment of welfare systems and his personal involvement in the well-being of the disadvantaged, Omar set a standard for governance that prioritized social justice and the protection of those most in need.

One of Omar's most significant contributions to the Islamic state was the creation of the **Bayt al-Mal**, or public treasury. The Bayt al-Mal served as a central institution for managing the resources of the Islamic state, and Omar made sure that a large portion of its funds was dedicated to supporting the poor, orphans, widows, and other vulnerable groups. Under his leadership, the public treasury became a means of redistributing wealth and ensuring that the wealth of the growing Islamic empire benefited all, not just the elite. Omar's establishment of this welfare system was revolutionary in its time, reflecting his deep understanding that a just society must care for its weakest members.

Omar's concern for the vulnerable went beyond policy. He took personal responsibility for the well-being of those in need. It is reported that he would often walk the streets of Medina at night, sometimes in disguise, to check on the conditions of the people. In one famous story, Omar overheard a widow struggling to feed her children. Without revealing his identity, he returned to the treasury, gathered food, and delivered it to her himself. When one of his companions offered to carry the load for him, Omar responded, "Will you carry my burden on the Day of Judgment?" This story highlights not only his empathy but also his belief that leadership is a responsibility that extends to ensuring the welfare of every individual under his care.

Omar also established specific programs aimed at protecting the rights and dignity of **orphans and widows**. He recognized that these groups were particularly vulnerable in society, often lacking the support needed to survive. To address this, Omar ensured that orphans received financial assistance from the state, allowing them to be cared for and educated. Widows were provided with stipends from the treasury, ensuring that they were not left destitute after the loss of their husbands. These policies reflected Omar's understanding that leadership required not only maintaining order and security but also creating a safety net for those who could not care for themselves.

In addition to financial support, Omar's compassion extended to the **fair treatment of the vulnerable in legal matters**. He was known for his insistence that orphans and widows be treated fairly in matters of inheritance and legal disputes. He closely monitored the application of Islamic law to ensure that their rights were upheld and that they were not exploited by others. Omar's dedication to justice and fairness was deeply intertwined with his empathy for those who were often overlooked or marginalized in society.

Omar's compassion for the vulnerable was also evident in times of crisis. During periods of famine and drought, Omar took extraordinary measures to ensure that no one went hungry. He ordered food to be distributed from the state reserves, often personally overseeing the distribution of resources to make sure that the poor were cared for. Omar himself lived modestly during these times, refusing to eat more than what was available to the poorest members of society. His self-imposed austerity during such crises demonstrated his deep empathy and his commitment to leading by example.

In conclusion, Omar ibn al-Khattab's leadership was characterized by his deep compassion for the vulnerable, particularly the poor, orphans, and widows. Through the establishment of welfare systems, personal acts of charity, and legal protections, Omar ensured that the Islamic state provided for those in need. His empathy was not just an abstract principle but a guiding force that shaped his governance, creating a society where even the most vulnerable were cared for and respected. Omar's legacy serves as a powerful reminder that true leadership involves not only power and authority but also a deep sense of responsibility for the well-being of every member of society.

The Power of Empathy in Governance and Decision-Making

EMPATHY IS A CRITICAL yet often overlooked quality in leadership, particularly in governance. Modern leaders who prioritize empathy in their decision-making processes are better equipped to create policies that serve the true needs of their people, foster trust, and maintain social harmony. Omar ibn al-Khattab (may Allah be pleased with him) demonstrated the power of empathy in his leadership by consistently putting the welfare of the most vulnerable at the center of his governance. His concern for the poor, orphans, and widows, as well as his personal involvement in their well-being, provides a powerful lesson for today's leaders about the importance of understanding the needs of others and incorporating compassion into decision-making.

Empathy allows leaders to make decisions that are **people-focused**. Rather than being driven solely by political, economic, or strategic interests, empathetic leaders consider the real-world impact of their decisions on individuals and communities. Omar's leadership was defined by his ability to connect with the everyday struggles of his people. His establishment of welfare systems and personal efforts to ensure that no one was left in need were rooted in his deep understanding of their hardships. Modern leaders can learn from this by making an effort to engage with and listen to those they serve, ensuring that their policies address the needs of all segments of society, particularly the marginalized.

Empathy also plays a crucial role in **building trust between leaders and the people**. When leaders demonstrate that they genuinely care about the welfare of their citizens, they earn trust and loyalty. Omar's nighttime walks through the streets of Medina, where he would check on the conditions of the people, showcased his deep concern for their well-being. His actions were not performative; they were motivated by a sincere desire to ensure that no one went hungry or was mistreated. Modern leaders who take the time to engage with their communities and show genuine care for their challenges create an environment where people feel valued and heard. This trust is essential for maintaining social cohesion and stability, particularly in times of crisis or change.

In governance, **empathy leads to more effective and sustainable policies**. When leaders understand the root causes of social issues, they are better positioned to create solutions that address these problems at their core. Omar's decision to create a public treasury (*Bayt al-Mal*) to support the poor, orphans, and widows was not only an act of compassion but also a practical solution to ensure long-term social stability. By addressing the needs of the vulnerable, Omar's policies helped prevent social unrest and created a more equitable society. Modern leaders can apply this lesson by focusing on policies that not only provide immediate relief but also create long-term solutions to systemic issues such as poverty, inequality, and access to essential services.

Empathy in leadership also fosters a culture of **inclusion and fairness**. Leaders who prioritize empathy are more likely to ensure that everyone, regardless of their social or economic status, has access to opportunities and resources. Omar's governance was marked by his insistence that the rights of orphans, widows, and the poor be protected and that they be treated with dignity. In modern governance, empathy helps leaders create inclusive policies that consider the needs of diverse populations, including marginalized and underserved communities. This inclusiveness not only strengthens social bonds but also ensures that everyone has a stake in the success of the society.

Another important aspect of empathy in leadership is its ability to **facilitate conflict resolution**. Leaders who understand the perspectives and emotions of others are better equipped to mediate conflicts and find common ground. Omar's ability to resolve disputes and administer justice was enhanced by his empathetic approach to leadership. He was able to see beyond the surface of issues and understand the deeper concerns of those involved, allowing him to make fair and balanced decisions. Modern leaders who practice empathy in conflict resolution can navigate disputes with a greater understanding of the underlying issues, leading to more peaceful and constructive outcomes.

In conclusion, empathy is not a weakness in leadership; it is a strength that allows leaders to make informed, compassionate, and effective decisions. Omar ibn al-Khattab's leadership demonstrates how empathy can shape governance in a way that prioritizes the well-being of the people, fosters trust, and creates a more just society. Modern leaders can learn from his example by incorporating empathy into their decision-making processes, engaging with their communities, creating inclusive policies, and addressing the needs of the most vulnerable. In doing so, they can lead with compassion and wisdom, ensuring that their leadership serves the greater good.

Practical Ways for Modern Leaders to Show Empathy and Implement Social Welfare Programs

EMPATHY IS ESSENTIAL in leadership, particularly when it comes to addressing the needs of society's most vulnerable populations. Modern leaders who prioritize empathy can create lasting change by implementing social welfare programs that provide critical support to those in need. Omar ibn al-Khattab's (may Allah be pleased with him) leadership provides a timeless example of how empathy can guide effective governance, especially through his establishment of welfare systems for the poor, orphans, and widows. For today's leaders, there are several practical ways to integrate empathy into decision-making and create comprehensive social welfare programs that benefit the entire community.

One of the most effective ways modern leaders can show empathy is by **engaging directly with the communities they serve**. This involves not only gathering data but also visiting communities, listening to their concerns, and understanding the challenges they face.

Omar's habit of walking through the streets of Medina to observe and address the needs of the people set a powerful example of a leader who took the time to connect with his community. Modern leaders can replicate this by holding town hall meetings, conducting surveys, and having direct dialogues with people from different socio-economic backgrounds. This hands-on approach helps leaders understand the real issues affecting their constituents and allows for more responsive and effective policymaking.

Another practical way to show empathy is through the **creation of targeted social welfare programs** that address the specific needs of vulnerable groups. Just as Omar established the Bayt al-Mal to ensure that resources were allocated to the poor, orphans, and widows, modern leaders can develop programs that provide direct support to marginalized populations. This could include cash transfer programs for low-income families, housing assistance, food security initiatives, and healthcare subsidies for those who cannot afford medical care. These programs should be designed to reach those who are most in need, with a focus on reducing economic inequality and providing a safety net for the disadvantaged.

Establishing social safety nets is another key way to implement empathetic leadership. Social safety nets, such as unemployment benefits, health insurance programs, and child welfare services, provide a foundation of security for individuals and families during times of hardship. These programs are particularly important in times of economic downturn or crisis. Omar's leadership during periods of famine and drought, when he personally ensured that food was distributed to those in need, reflects the importance of protecting the most vulnerable during times of distress. Modern leaders can apply this by strengthening and expanding social welfare programs that ensure no one is left without basic support during difficult times.

Leaders can also **integrate empathy into their decision-making processes** by using data to identify and address systemic inequalities.

This involves analyzing data on poverty rates, access to healthcare, education, and employment opportunities to develop targeted interventions that address the root causes of inequality. Omar's approach to governance, where he carefully monitored the distribution of resources and ensured that the vulnerable were not overlooked, serves as a model for how data-driven policies can create more equitable outcomes. By using data to inform decisions, modern leaders can allocate resources more effectively and ensure that social welfare programs are reaching those who need them the most.

Collaboration with non-governmental organizations (NGOs), charities, and community groups is another practical way for modern leaders to show empathy and implement social welfare programs. These organizations often have deep ties to local communities and can provide valuable insights into the specific needs of vulnerable populations. By partnering with these groups, leaders can expand the reach and effectiveness of social welfare initiatives. For example, leaders could work with food banks, homeless shelters, or educational organizations to provide services that complement government welfare programs. Omar's engagement with his community, particularly his personal involvement in charity, underscores the importance of collaboration in meeting the needs of society.

Modern leaders can also **ensure that social welfare programs are inclusive and accessible** by removing barriers that prevent people from accessing the support they need. This includes simplifying application processes for welfare benefits, providing assistance to non-native speakers, and ensuring that services are available to people with disabilities. Omar's leadership was characterized by his emphasis on fairness and justice, ensuring that all people—regardless of their status—were treated with dignity and given equal access to resources. In a similar vein, modern leaders should focus on making social welfare programs user-friendly and accessible to all, particularly to those who may face difficulties navigating bureaucratic systems.

Finally, **leaders can lead by example** by personally demonstrating empathy and compassion in their daily actions. This could involve volunteering with social welfare organizations, donating to charitable causes, or using their platform to advocate for policies that support the vulnerable. Omar's personal acts of charity, such as delivering food to families in need and ensuring the fair treatment of orphans, showed that leadership is not just about creating policies but also about embodying the values of empathy and service. Modern leaders can follow his example by taking visible, concrete actions that demonstrate their commitment to the well-being of the people they serve.

In conclusion, modern leaders can show empathy in governance by engaging directly with communities, creating targeted social welfare programs, establishing social safety nets, using data to address inequality, collaborating with NGOs, ensuring accessibility, and leading by example. Omar ibn al-Khattab's leadership provides a powerful model for how empathy can guide effective decision-making and the implementation of social welfare programs that uplift society's most vulnerable members. By applying these principles, modern leaders can foster a more compassionate and equitable society.

Chapter 9: Visionary Leadership: Shaping the Future Through Lasting Reforms

Omar ibn al-Khattab (may Allah be pleased with him) was not only a leader of the present but also a visionary who laid the foundations for a future that would benefit generations to come. His leadership was marked by foresight, strategic thinking, and a commitment to building enduring systems that strengthened the Islamic state. Omar's ability to implement long-term reforms in administration, governance, and military organization is a testament to his visionary leadership. His introduction of the Islamic calendar and numerous structural reforms helped shape a lasting legacy that influenced not only his contemporaries but also the future course of Islamic civilization.

One of Omar's most significant contributions was his **administrative reforms**, which streamlined the governance of the rapidly expanding Islamic empire. Recognizing the need for efficient management, Omar established a formal administrative structure that included the creation of various government departments responsible for taxation, finance, public works, and the military. This system ensured that the empire's growing wealth and resources were managed effectively, benefiting the entire community. His development of the **diwan** system—essentially a registry of soldiers and public servants—ensured that the distribution of resources, including stipends and pensions, was organized and fair. This kind of foresight in governance enabled the Islamic state to manage its rapid expansion and maintain stability over time.

Omar's **introduction of the Islamic calendar** was another example of his visionary thinking. By formalizing the Islamic calendar, based on the Hijra (the migration of the Prophet Muhammad, peace be upon him, from Mecca to Medina), Omar provided the Muslim community with a unified system of timekeeping. This decision was not only practical—enabling consistency in legal and administrative matters such as taxation, trade, and religious observances—but also symbolic. The calendar marked the Islamic community's identity and reinforced the significance of the Hijra in shaping the Muslim ummah (community). This innovation had lasting effects on the cohesion of the Muslim world, as it provided a common framework for governance, worship, and historical record.

Omar's visionary leadership extended to **military organization** as well. As the Islamic empire expanded, Omar recognized the need for a well-structured military force to protect the state's borders and ensure internal stability. He reorganized the military by establishing permanent army bases, developing a system of regular payments for soldiers, and ensuring that military campaigns were meticulously planned and executed. His reforms in military administration allowed the Islamic state to maintain a highly effective and disciplined army, even as it rapidly conquered new territories. By investing in the long-term sustainability of the military, Omar ensured that the Islamic empire was not only secure but also capable of defending itself against future threats.

The lesson from Omar's leadership for modern leaders is clear: **visionary leadership builds enduring systems** that benefit future generations. Leaders who think beyond immediate challenges and focus on long-term goals create a lasting impact that extends far beyond their tenure. Omar's reforms in administration, the military, and the establishment of the Islamic calendar demonstrate that leaders must anticipate the future needs of their society and take proactive steps to address them. His ability to see the bigger picture allowed him to create systems that continued to function effectively long after his time as caliph.

For modern leaders, this means that visionary leadership involves **strategic planning and long-term thinking**. Leaders must not only address current issues but also consider the future implications of their decisions. By focusing on building strong institutions, leaders can create structures that support societal progress over time. Just as Omar's administrative reforms ensured the efficient management of the Islamic state, modern leaders can focus on establishing systems that provide for the long-term well-being of their communities, whether through education, infrastructure development, or economic policy.

Another key aspect of visionary leadership is the ability to **innovate and adapt** to changing circumstances. Omar's introduction of the Islamic calendar and his military reforms were innovations designed to meet the evolving needs of the Islamic state. Modern leaders can apply this lesson by being open to new ideas and willing to implement reforms that address emerging challenges. Whether it's incorporating new technologies, creating policies that promote sustainability, or preparing for shifts in the global economy, visionary leaders must be willing to adapt and innovate in order to secure a prosperous future.

Visionary leadership also requires a focus on **building institutions that promote social justice and equity**. Omar's reforms were not only about maintaining control but also about ensuring that wealth and resources were distributed fairly. His establishment of the public treasury and the diwan system ensured that the needs of all members of society, particularly the vulnerable, were met. Modern leaders can follow this example by creating policies and institutions that promote fairness and inclusivity, ensuring that future generations inherit a society built on the principles of justice and equality.

In conclusion, Omar ibn al-Khattab's leadership exemplifies the power of visionary thinking in creating lasting systems that benefit future generations. His administrative reforms, military organization, and introduction of the Islamic calendar showcase how a leader's ability to think ahead and implement long-term strategies can shape the future of a society. Modern leaders can learn from Omar's example by focusing on strategic planning, being open to innovation, and building institutions that promote social justice. By adopting a visionary approach, today's leaders can create a legacy that endures and ensures the prosperity and well-being of future generations.

Omar's Long-Term Vision: Administrative Reforms, the Islamic Calendar, and Military Organization

OMAR IBN AL-KHATTAB (may Allah be pleased with him) was not only a leader focused on addressing the immediate needs of the growing Islamic empire, but he also had a clear and far-reaching vision for the future. His leadership was characterized by strategic reforms and innovations that laid the foundation for the Islamic state's continued growth and stability long after his tenure as caliph. Omar's long-term vision is most evident in his administrative reforms, the introduction of the Islamic calendar, and his reorganization of the military. These initiatives were not merely reactive to the challenges of the time but were designed to ensure the sustainability and prosperity of the Islamic empire for generations to come.

One of Omar's most significant contributions was his **administrative reforms**, which streamlined governance and created a more efficient system for managing the rapidly expanding Islamic empire. As the territories under Islamic control grew, Omar recognized the need for a formal administrative structure to maintain order and ensure that the resources of the state were properly managed. To address this, he established various government departments responsible for overseeing finance, taxation, public works, and military affairs. This division of responsibilities allowed for better coordination and accountability, ensuring that the wealth of the empire was distributed fairly and used for the common good.

Omar's creation of the **diwan system** was particularly impactful. The diwan was essentially a registry of public officials, soldiers, and other state employees, allowing for the organized distribution of salaries and pensions. This system not only ensured that the military and public servants were compensated fairly but also provided a means of redistributing wealth across the empire. Omar's administrative reforms helped create a stable and transparent governance system that could effectively manage the empire's resources, contributing to its long-term sustainability.

Another example of Omar's long-term vision was his **introduction of the Islamic calendar**. In 638 CE, Omar formalized the Islamic calendar, which was based on the lunar year and began with the Hijra, the migration of the Prophet Muhammad (peace be upon him) from Mecca to Medina. This decision was more than just a practical solution for timekeeping; it was a unifying force for the Muslim community. The Islamic calendar provided consistency in legal and administrative matters, such as the collection of taxes and the observance of religious events. It also reinforced the significance of the Hijra as a foundational moment in Islamic history, strengthening the Muslim identity and sense of shared purpose.

By establishing the Islamic calendar, Omar ensured that the Muslim community had a standardized system for marking time, which was crucial for governance and religious observance. This innovation allowed for greater coordination across the growing empire, as everyone followed the same calendar, whether they were in Medina, Damascus, or Cairo. The adoption of the Islamic calendar was a forward-thinking move that demonstrated Omar's understanding of the importance of unity and organization in maintaining a strong and cohesive state.

Omar's **reorganization of the military** was another key element of his long-term vision. As the Islamic empire expanded through military conquests, Omar recognized the need for a well-structured and professional army to defend the empire's borders and maintain internal stability. He implemented reforms that transformed the military into a more permanent and disciplined force. One of the most significant changes was the establishment of military bases in key regions, ensuring that troops were strategically positioned to respond quickly to threats.

Omar also introduced a system of regular payments for soldiers, which was recorded in the diwan. This ensured that the army was not only well-funded but also loyal and motivated, as soldiers were compensated for their service. Additionally, Omar made sure that the military campaigns were carefully planned and that the resources of the state were used efficiently. His emphasis on strategic planning and military organization ensured that the Islamic empire remained secure and that its military strength could be sustained over the long term.

Omar's military reforms were not solely focused on expanding the empire but on protecting it from future threats. By establishing a strong and organized military force, Omar ensured that the Islamic state would be able to defend its borders and maintain peace within its territories. This forward-thinking approach helped create a sense of security and stability, which contributed to the empire's long-term success.

In conclusion, Omar ibn al-Khattab's long-term vision for the Islamic state was evident in his administrative reforms, the introduction of the Islamic calendar, and his reorganization of the military. These initiatives were designed not only to address the challenges of his time but also to ensure the stability, prosperity, and unity of the Islamic empire for future generations. Omar's ability to think beyond the immediate needs of the state and implement lasting reforms that benefited society as a whole demonstrates the power of visionary leadership. His legacy serves as a reminder that true leadership is about building systems and institutions that endure, providing a strong foundation for the future.

The Power of Visionary Leadership: Building Systems for Future Generations

VISIONARY LEADERSHIP is not just about addressing the challenges of today; it is about anticipating the needs of tomorrow and building systems that will endure for future generations. Leaders who think long-term and focus on creating sustainable, adaptable structures leave a lasting impact that benefits their societies long after they are gone. Omar ibn al-Khattab (may Allah be pleased with him) exemplified this type of leadership, particularly through his administrative reforms, introduction of the Islamic calendar, and reorganization of the military. His forward-thinking approach ensured that the Islamic empire remained strong, efficient, and unified, even as it faced rapid expansion and new challenges.

For modern leaders, Omar's example demonstrates that **visionary leadership requires creating enduring systems** that can adapt to changing circumstances while providing stability. One of the key components of visionary leadership is the ability to think beyond immediate gains and focus on building institutions that can withstand the test of time. Omar's establishment of the diwan system, which organized the distribution of wealth, salaries, and resources, is a perfect illustration of this. By creating a formal structure for managing the empire's finances, Omar ensured that future leaders could maintain a fair and efficient system of governance, regardless of external pressures or internal changes.

Visionary leaders also recognize the importance of unifying principles and frameworks that bind people together. Omar's introduction of the Islamic calendar is an example of how leaders can create systems that not only address practical needs but also foster a sense of identity and unity among their people. The Islamic calendar provided a standardized way to manage time across the empire, while also reinforcing the shared religious and cultural values of the Muslim community. Modern leaders can apply this lesson by developing policies or systems that serve both functional purposes and cultural or symbolic roles, ensuring that their leadership strengthens the social fabric of their communities.

Another essential aspect of visionary leadership is the **ability to plan for long-term security and stability**. Omar's military reforms, which professionalized the army and established military bases across the empire, were designed to protect the Islamic state not just in his time but for future generations. By creating a disciplined and well-organized military force, Omar ensured that the empire could defend itself against external threats and maintain internal order. Modern leaders can learn from this by focusing on building strong, resilient institutions—whether in defense, education, infrastructure, or healthcare—that are equipped to handle future challenges. These institutions should be designed with flexibility in mind, allowing them to evolve as new threats or opportunities arise.

Visionary leadership also involves **building systems that promote fairness and inclusivity**. Omar's emphasis on justice, particularly in the treatment of orphans, widows, and the poor, shows that enduring systems must be built on principles of fairness. His creation of social welfare programs ensured that the most vulnerable members of society were cared for, regardless of their status or background. Modern leaders can apply this lesson by developing policies and institutions that prioritize social equity, ensuring that all members of society have access to opportunities and resources. Leaders who build systems based on fairness create societies that are more stable and cohesive, as people feel valued and included.

Finally, visionary leadership requires a **focus on sustainability and adaptability**. Systems that are rigid or short-sighted may work for a time, but they often collapse under the weight of future challenges. Omar's ability to adapt the governance of the Islamic empire to its rapid expansion—by implementing administrative reforms, reorganizing the military, and introducing a standardized calendar—ensured that the state could continue to function effectively even as it grew. Modern leaders must similarly focus on creating systems that can adapt to future economic, social, or environmental changes. This may involve incorporating technology, investing in education, or promoting innovation within institutions to ensure their longevity.

In conclusion, visionary leadership is about creating systems that endure and adapt over time, benefiting not just the current generation but also those that follow. Omar ibn al-Khattab's leadership provides a powerful example of how long-term thinking, strategic planning, and a commitment to fairness can build strong, sustainable institutions. Modern leaders can learn from his example by focusing on the future, building systems that promote unity, security, fairness, and adaptability, and ensuring that their leadership leaves a lasting legacy that benefits society for generations to come.

Creating and Implementing Long-Term Strategies for Societal Progress

EFFECTIVE LEADERS UNDERSTAND that true progress is not achieved overnight but requires thoughtful planning, patience, and a long-term vision. Leaders who focus on building sustainable systems and strategies can create lasting positive change that benefits future generations. Omar ibn al-Khattab (may Allah be pleased with him) demonstrated this approach through his reforms, which laid the groundwork for the continued success of the Islamic state. Modern leaders can apply similar principles by creating and implementing long-term strategies that address the needs of their societies while anticipating future challenges.

The first step in creating long-term strategies is for leaders to **define a clear vision for the future**. This vision should encompass not only the immediate goals of the organization, state, or community but also broader objectives that will shape the society for years to come. Leaders need to ask themselves what kind of legacy they want to leave behind and what long-term impact they wish to have. Omar's introduction of administrative reforms and the Islamic calendar demonstrated his focus on building systems that would ensure the unity and sustainability of the Islamic state. Modern leaders should similarly develop a vision that looks beyond the current challenges and focuses on creating institutions that will serve future generations.

Once a vision is established, leaders must focus on **building strong and adaptable institutions**. Institutions are the backbone of any society, and their strength determines the society's ability to thrive in the long term. Omar's administrative reforms, which created a formal structure for managing finances, public works, and military affairs, ensured that the Islamic state could function efficiently even as it expanded. Modern leaders should prioritize building institutions that are not only effective today but also capable of evolving as society changes. This might involve establishing new educational systems, healthcare programs, or economic policies that can adapt to future technological, demographic, or environmental shifts.

Investing in education and human capital is another essential component of long-term societal progress. Leaders must recognize that the future prosperity of their society depends on the skills, knowledge, and innovation of its people. Omar's emphasis on justice and fair governance extended to ensuring that all members of society, including the vulnerable, had the opportunity to thrive. Modern leaders can follow his example by investing in education systems that promote critical thinking, innovation, and inclusivity. By creating opportunities for people to develop their talents and contribute to society, leaders can foster a culture of progress that will continue to grow over time.

Developing policies that promote social equity and fairness is also critical for long-term success. Societies that fail to address inequality and injustice are prone to instability and division. Omar's welfare programs and efforts to protect the rights of the poor, orphans, and widows are examples of how leaders can create systems that ensure fairness for all members of society. Modern leaders can implement long-term strategies that focus on reducing economic inequality, expanding access to healthcare and education, and ensuring that all citizens have equal opportunities to succeed. By addressing systemic inequities, leaders can build more cohesive and resilient societies that are better equipped to face future challenges.

To implement long-term strategies, leaders must also focus on **creating sustainable economic policies**. This involves building a robust economy that can withstand external shocks, while also promoting innovation and technological advancement. Leaders should focus on diversifying their economies, investing in infrastructure, and supporting industries that will drive future growth. Omar's reforms ensured that the Islamic state had the financial and military resources necessary to maintain stability and protect its borders. Modern leaders can similarly focus on building resilient economies that provide a strong foundation for future prosperity.

Collaboration and consensus-building are also crucial for the successful implementation of long-term strategies. Leaders must engage with diverse stakeholders, including government officials, community leaders, and citizens, to ensure that their policies reflect the needs and aspirations of the broader population. Omar's practice of consulting his companions and seeking their advice before making important decisions exemplified the value of collaboration in leadership. Modern leaders should work to build consensus around their long-term vision and ensure that their strategies have broad support. This collaborative approach not only strengthens the legitimacy of leadership but also ensures that long-term strategies are more likely to succeed.

Finally, leaders must be willing to **adapt and innovate** as circumstances change. No long-term strategy can account for every potential challenge, and leaders must remain flexible and open to revising their plans when necessary. Omar's ability to adapt his military strategies and governance structures as the Islamic empire expanded showed his willingness to adjust his approach when needed. Modern leaders should foster a culture of innovation within their organizations or societies, encouraging continuous improvement and openness to new ideas. This adaptability ensures that long-term strategies remain relevant and effective, even as new challenges arise.

In conclusion, creating and implementing long-term strategies for societal progress requires a clear vision, strong institutions, investment in education and human capital, policies that promote social equity, sustainable economic development, collaboration, and a willingness to adapt. By applying these principles, modern leaders can create lasting systems that ensure the prosperity and well-being of their societies for generations to come. Omar ibn al-Khattab's leadership serves as a powerful model for how visionary thinking and long-term planning can shape the future in ways that benefit all members of society.

Part IV: Rule of Law and Forgiveness: Balancing Justice with Compassion in Leadership

A truly great leader understands that governance is not solely about power and authority; it is about maintaining justice and fostering unity within society. Omar ibn al-Khattab (may Allah be pleased with him) embodied these principles by upholding the rule of law with unwavering commitment while also practicing forgiveness and patience in moments of conflict. His leadership demonstrated a deep understanding of the balance between enforcing justice and extending mercy, which created an environment of fairness and stability. In the modern world, these qualities remain essential for leaders who seek to govern effectively, maintaining order while also promoting reconciliation and harmony.

Omar's dedication to the **rule of law** was one of the defining features of his leadership. He was known for his impartiality in administering justice, ensuring that no one, regardless of their social status or familial ties, was above the law. Omar believed that a society could only be stable and just if its leaders held themselves accountable to the same standards as everyone else. This commitment to justice extended even to his own family members, as Omar once famously punished his own son for breaking the law. His enforcement of the rule of law reinforced the idea that fairness and equality are essential for building trust within a society, and that leaders must lead by example when it comes to upholding justice.

Equally important was Omar's capacity for **forgiveness and patience**. Despite his firm commitment to justice, Omar also recognized that leadership requires the ability to forgive and show patience, especially in difficult situations. He understood that conflicts often arise within any community and that resolution is not always achieved through strict punishment or retribution. Instead, Omar demonstrated the importance of reconciliation, seeking peaceful solutions and showing mercy whenever possible. His ability to forgive, even when it might have been easier to punish, made him a beloved leader and helped maintain unity within the Islamic state. For Omar, leadership was not only about enforcing the law but also about showing compassion, which in turn strengthened the bonds within the community.

This part of the book will explore how modern leaders can apply the principles of the **rule of law and forgiveness** to create just, stable, and harmonious societies. By delving into Omar's example, we will examine how a leader can be both a firm enforcer of justice and a compassionate agent of peace, understanding that these qualities are not mutually exclusive but rather complementary aspects of effective leadership.

Chapter 10: Commitment to the Rule of Law: Justice Above All

Omar ibn al-Khattab (may Allah be pleased with him) was known for his unwavering commitment to the rule of law, a cornerstone of his leadership. He understood that a just society could not thrive unless everyone, regardless of their status or position, was held accountable to the same legal standards. His administration of justice was marked by impartiality, ensuring that even the most powerful individuals, including his own family, were not exempt from the law. This firm belief in equality before the law helped solidify his reputation as a leader of integrity and fairness, and it played a crucial role in the stability and success of the early Islamic state.

Omar's dedication to the rule of law can be seen in several instances during his caliphate. One of the most notable examples was when his son committed a crime, and Omar insisted that the full weight of the law be applied, despite the familial connection. Omar's refusal to show favoritism, even in such a personal matter, highlighted his belief that justice must be blind to personal ties or social status. He viewed the law as a sacred institution that was above individuals, including those in positions of power. This impartial application of justice not only preserved the integrity of the legal system but also reinforced the public's trust in his leadership.

For modern leaders, Omar's example offers a crucial lesson: **upholding the rule of law is essential for ensuring justice and stability** within any society. When leaders apply the law consistently and without bias, they build a culture of fairness that fosters trust and social cohesion. In contrast, when laws are applied unevenly or selectively, it leads to disillusionment, corruption, and instability. People lose faith in the system when they see that certain individuals or groups are above the law, leading to divisions and resentment. Omar's leadership serves as a reminder that true justice requires impartiality and that laws must be enforced consistently, regardless of the individuals involved.

To strengthen the rule of law, modern leaders can take several practical steps. First, **establishing transparent legal frameworks** is essential. Laws must be clear, accessible, and understood by all members of society. Leaders should ensure that the legal system is transparent and that legal proceedings are open and fair. This helps build trust in the system and ensures that all citizens, regardless of their status, know that they will be treated fairly under the law.

Second, leaders must **lead by example** when it comes to following the law. Just as Omar held himself and his family to the same legal standards as everyone else, modern leaders must demonstrate that they are not above the law. This requires leaders to be accountable for their actions and to accept the consequences of any wrongdoing, no matter their position. When leaders show that they are subject to the same laws as ordinary citizens, it strengthens the public's belief in the fairness of the legal system.

Another way to strengthen the rule of law is by ensuring that **law enforcement and judicial systems are independent and free from corruption**. Omar's commitment to justice included appointing judges and officials who were known for their integrity and fairness. Modern leaders can follow this example by promoting judicial independence, ensuring that law enforcement agencies are not influenced by political pressures or personal interests. This prevents corruption and ensures that legal decisions are based on merit rather than favoritism or coercion.

Finally, modern leaders can **promote equality before the law** by addressing systemic biases that exist within legal frameworks. This may involve reforming laws that disproportionately affect marginalized communities or ensuring that all individuals, regardless of race, gender, or economic status, have access to legal representation and justice. Leaders must be vigilant in identifying and addressing any inequalities that exist within the legal system, as these inequalities erode trust and weaken the rule of law.

In conclusion, Omar ibn al-Khattab's commitment to the rule of law serves as a powerful example of how justice can be upheld with fairness and impartiality. Modern leaders can learn from his leadership by focusing on transparency, accountability, judicial independence, and equality before the law. By strengthening the rule of law, leaders not only ensure justice but also create a stable and cohesive society where all individuals are treated with fairness and respect.

Omar's Impartial Enforcement of the Rule of Law: Justice Above All

OMAR IBN AL-KHATTAB (may Allah be pleased with him) was a leader whose unwavering commitment to justice became the cornerstone of his leadership. One of the defining characteristics of his caliphate was his strict enforcement of the rule of law, ensuring that no one, regardless of their status, influence, or familial connection, was above the law. Omar believed that true justice required impartiality, and he applied the law without exception, even when it involved his own family members or close companions. This impartiality became a hallmark of his governance, creating a legacy of fairness and trust in the legal system.

Omar's belief in the **equality of all before the law** was demonstrated through several key moments during his leadership. One of the most notable instances involved his son, who had committed a crime. Rather than offering leniency or special treatment, Omar insisted that his son face the same punishment as anyone else who had broken the law. This decision, though difficult on a personal level, was a clear message to the community: the law was not subject to personal influence or favoritism. For Omar, justice was not negotiable, and it was crucial that even his own family be held accountable under the same standards as everyone else.

Omar's application of justice was not only directed at individuals but also at the powerful elites within society. He was known for holding governors, military leaders, and other officials accountable for their actions, ensuring that their authority did not exempt them from the laws of the land. In one famous case, a governor was accused of mistreating the people under his care, and Omar promptly removed him from his position despite the governor's high standing. This impartial approach to justice reinforced the public's confidence in Omar's leadership and established him as a leader who placed justice above personal relationships or political alliances.

Another example of Omar's commitment to fairness was his treatment of non-Muslims living under Islamic rule. Omar ensured that Christians, Jews, and other religious minorities were treated with justice and respect, and he protected their rights under Islamic law. His enforcement of the rule of law extended to all citizens, regardless of their faith, reflecting his deep commitment to creating a society based on justice and equality. This approach not only strengthened the Islamic state but also fostered social cohesion among its diverse population.

Omar's strict and impartial enforcement of the law was not without challenges. He often faced criticism or pressure from those who expected leniency or special treatment due to their status or relationship with him. However, Omar's steadfastness in upholding justice never wavered. He believed that a just society required leaders who would apply the law fairly, regardless of external pressures. His leadership demonstrated that the rule of law must be applied equally to all if trust in governance and social order is to be maintained.

Omar's commitment to the rule of law is a powerful example for modern leaders. His belief that no one was above the law created a culture of accountability that not only upheld justice but also ensured the stability of the Islamic state. By applying the law impartially, Omar set a precedent for fairness in leadership and established a legacy that would be remembered for generations.

In conclusion, Omar ibn al-Khattab's impartial enforcement of the rule of law serves as a timeless example of how justice must be applied equally to all, regardless of status or relationship. His leadership demonstrated the importance of holding everyone accountable to the same legal standards, ensuring that no one, including the most powerful individuals, was above the law. This commitment to fairness and justice was key to his success as a leader and remains a model for governance in modern times.

The Critical Importance of Upholding the Rule of Law for Justice and Stability

UPHOLDING THE RULE of law is one of the most fundamental responsibilities of any leader. It ensures that justice is applied fairly and consistently, and that society functions in an orderly, stable manner. When leaders are committed to enforcing laws impartially and transparently, they foster trust, promote fairness, and maintain stability. Omar ibn al-Khattab (may Allah be pleased with him) understood this deeply and made the rule of law a central principle of his governance. His impartial enforcement of justice, regardless of personal ties or status, created a strong, cohesive society built on mutual trust and respect for the law. For modern leaders, the rule of law is equally crucial, as it lays the foundation for a just and stable society.

Justice depends on the rule of law because it ensures that laws are applied equally to everyone, without bias or favoritism. A system where some people are exempt from legal consequences due to their wealth, power, or influence creates deep divisions and erodes public trust. Omar demonstrated how important it is for leaders to hold everyone accountable, even if that means punishing their own family members. His unwavering commitment to justice was based on the belief that the law must be applied to all citizens equally, without regard to their status. Modern leaders must follow this example, ensuring that no one is above the law and that justice is served impartially.

When the rule of law is consistently upheld, **society becomes more stable**. Stability arises from the predictability and fairness of legal systems. People feel secure when they know that laws are enforced fairly and consistently, and that they are protected by the same rules as everyone else. Omar's leadership showed how the consistent enforcement of laws, applied to all citizens regardless of their background, created a stable and harmonious society. Without the rule of law, societies often fall into chaos or authoritarianism, where laws are used selectively, and people's rights are easily violated. For modern leaders, upholding the rule of law creates a sense of security and social order, which is essential for long-term stability.

Moreover, the rule of law is crucial for **preventing corruption and abuse of power**. When leaders enforce laws impartially, they prevent those in power from using their influence for personal gain. Omar's approach to justice demonstrated that even powerful individuals, such as governors and military leaders, were not exempt from the law. By holding officials accountable, Omar helped to build a culture of integrity and fairness within the Islamic state. Modern leaders can learn from this by ensuring that laws apply equally to those in positions of power, preventing corruption, favoritism, and the misuse of authority. This, in turn, strengthens trust in leadership and governance.

The rule of law also ensures **equality before the law**, promoting fairness in society. When leaders ensure that laws are applied equally to all, it creates a sense of fairness and social cohesion. Citizens are more likely to respect laws when they know that everyone, from the wealthiest to the poorest, is subject to the same legal standards. Omar's insistence on equality before the law, regardless of one's position or family, fostered a sense of unity and respect within his society. Modern leaders can achieve similar results by making sure that legal systems do not favor certain groups or individuals, but rather promote fairness and equal treatment for all citizens.

In conclusion, upholding the rule of law is essential for creating a just and stable society. Leaders who enforce laws impartially, ensure equality before the law, and prevent corruption lay the foundation for trust and social harmony. Omar ibn al-Khattab's leadership exemplified the importance of the rule of law in building a fair and stable society, and his legacy provides modern leaders with a powerful lesson in the value of justice. By committing to the rule of law, modern leaders can create societies where justice prevails, and stability is maintained, ensuring the well-being of all citizens.

Strengthening the Rule of Law and Ensuring Equality Before It

IN TODAY'S COMPLEX and rapidly changing world, modern leaders face the crucial task of reinforcing the rule of law and ensuring that all individuals, regardless of their background, are treated equally under it. The rule of law serves as the backbone of justice, promoting fairness and maintaining social order. Without it, societies risk falling into corruption, inequality, and instability. Omar ibn al-Khattab's (may Allah be pleased with him) leadership provides valuable insights into how modern leaders can uphold these principles by applying laws impartially and fostering trust in the legal system. By strengthening the rule of law, leaders can create societies where justice and equality are not just ideals but realities.

One of the most effective ways modern leaders can strengthen the rule of law is by **ensuring transparency and accountability in legal processes**. Legal systems must be open and clear to the public, allowing citizens to understand their rights and obligations. Leaders should advocate for legal reforms that make the justice system more transparent, such as publishing legal decisions, making court proceedings accessible, and ensuring that laws are written in clear, understandable language. Transparency in the legal system builds trust, as people are more likely to respect laws when they see that justice is administered openly and fairly. Omar's leadership exemplified this through his public hearings, where legal matters were discussed openly, and all parties were treated with respect and fairness.

Another important step is **promoting judicial independence**. For the rule of law to be strong, the judiciary must operate independently from political influence and external pressures. Omar appointed judges known for their integrity and fairness, ensuring that they could make decisions based solely on the law rather than personal or political considerations. Modern leaders can support judicial independence by ensuring that judges are appointed based on merit, protecting them from undue influence, and providing them with the resources they need to perform their duties effectively. This allows the legal system to function without bias, promoting impartiality and equality before the law.

Addressing systemic inequalities within the legal system is also crucial for ensuring that all citizens are treated equally. In many societies, marginalized groups—whether based on race, gender, religion, or socioeconomic status—face unequal treatment under the law. Modern leaders must work to identify and dismantle these systemic biases, ensuring that all individuals have access to justice. This may involve reforming discriminatory laws, ensuring legal representation for disadvantaged communities, and training law enforcement officials to recognize and eliminate biases in their work. Omar's commitment to justice extended to ensuring that non-Muslims living under Islamic rule were treated fairly and that their rights were protected. Modern leaders can follow his example by promoting fairness and equality for all members of society, regardless of their background.

Leaders should also **hold law enforcement and public officials accountable** for their actions. One of the key elements of a strong rule of law is ensuring that those tasked with enforcing the law are also subject to it. Omar demonstrated this by holding governors, military leaders, and even his own family members accountable for their actions under the law. Modern leaders can apply this by establishing clear mechanisms for investigating and addressing misconduct among law enforcement officers, government officials, and public servants. By enforcing accountability at every level, leaders ensure that the rule of law is upheld consistently, preventing abuse of power and maintaining public trust in the system.

Fostering a culture of legal literacy and public engagement is another vital step in strengthening the rule of law. Citizens need to understand their rights and responsibilities under the law to fully participate in the legal system. Leaders can promote legal literacy through public education campaigns, offering free legal advice clinics, and making legal resources more accessible to the public. When people understand their rights and how the legal system works, they are more likely to engage with it and seek justice when needed. Omar's leadership was characterized by his accessibility to the public, regularly engaging with people to ensure they understood and trusted the legal processes. Modern leaders should create opportunities for citizens to engage with the legal system and provide platforms for public participation in legal reforms.

Finally, modern leaders can strengthen the rule of law by **building coalitions with civil society organizations and advocacy groups**. These groups often play a critical role in holding governments accountable, pushing for legal reforms, and protecting the rights of marginalized communities. By working in collaboration with civil society, leaders can better understand the needs of different populations and implement laws that are fair and inclusive. Omar's governance was marked by his willingness to listen to the concerns of his people and adapt his policies accordingly. Similarly, modern leaders can foster stronger legal systems by maintaining open dialogues with civil society and ensuring that laws reflect the needs and rights of all citizens.

In conclusion, strengthening the rule of law and ensuring equality before it requires modern leaders to focus on transparency, judicial independence, accountability, and public engagement. By addressing systemic inequalities and promoting fairness, leaders can create legal systems that are trusted and respected by all citizens. Omar ibn al-Khattab's leadership offers a powerful example of how impartiality and accountability in the rule of law lead to justice and stability. By following these principles, modern leaders can build societies where justice prevails, and the rights of all citizens are protected equally under the law.

Chapter 11: Forgiveness and Patience: Keys to Conflict Resolution in Leadership

Leadership requires not only strength and decisiveness but also the capacity for forgiveness and patience, especially in times of conflict and tension. Omar ibn al-Khattab (may Allah be pleased with him) was known for his ability to balance justice with mercy, demonstrating great patience and a willingness to forgive even in the most difficult situations. His leadership was marked by a deep understanding that conflicts often require not just firm action but also a compassionate approach to achieve reconciliation and lasting peace. For modern leaders, the ability to practice forgiveness and exercise patience is critical for building trust, maintaining harmony, and resolving disputes in a constructive manner.

One of the most compelling aspects of Omar's leadership was his **willingness to forgive**, even when others expected harsh retribution. On numerous occasions, Omar showed restraint and patience when dealing with individuals who had wronged him or the state. He understood that leadership is not about seeking revenge but about promoting unity and peace. In one notable instance, a man who had spoken out against him publicly later came to ask for forgiveness. Instead of punishing him, Omar chose to forgive, demonstrating his belief in reconciliation over retribution. This act of forgiveness helped to heal divisions within the community and reinforced Omar's reputation as a just and compassionate leader.

Omar's **patience in leadership** was equally important. He often faced challenging situations that could have provoked anger or hasty decisions, but he consistently chose a measured approach. During times of crisis, such as famine or unrest, Omar displayed incredible patience, carefully considering the best course of action rather than reacting impulsively. His patience allowed him to weigh different perspectives, consult with his advisors, and ultimately make decisions that were in the best interest of the community. This approach not only prevented unnecessary conflict but also fostered a sense of stability and confidence among the people he led.

For modern leaders, Omar's example offers a valuable lesson: **forgiveness and patience are essential tools in resolving conflicts and maintaining peace**. Leadership often involves navigating difficult interpersonal dynamics and managing disputes, whether within organizations, governments, or communities. In such situations, a leader's ability to forgive and show patience can de-escalate tensions and open the door to reconciliation. Leaders who are quick to punish or retaliate risk deepening conflicts and alienating those they lead. Instead, by embracing forgiveness, leaders can create an environment where mistakes are acknowledged but not held against individuals, allowing for personal growth and stronger relationships.

Patience is equally crucial in leadership, especially when facing long-term challenges or crises. Impulsive decisions made in the heat of the moment often lead to regret, while patience allows leaders to think strategically and make decisions that have lasting positive effects. Omar's patience during crises, such as the severe drought during his caliphate, enabled him to manage resources wisely and prioritize the needs of the most vulnerable. Modern leaders can apply this lesson by practicing patience in decision-making, particularly in high-pressure situations, where a calm and thoughtful approach can lead to better outcomes for all.

To practice forgiveness and patience in leadership, modern leaders can start by **creating a culture of open communication and understanding**. By fostering an environment where individuals feel comfortable expressing their concerns and mistakes, leaders can more easily address conflicts before they escalate. Leaders can also model forgiveness by responding to errors or disagreements with empathy rather than punishment, showing that reconciliation and learning from mistakes are valued over assigning blame.

Leaders should also focus on **building emotional resilience**, which is essential for maintaining patience in difficult situations. Emotional resilience allows leaders to stay calm under pressure, respond thoughtfully to criticism, and avoid reacting out of frustration or anger. Developing resilience involves practicing mindfulness, stress management, and self-reflection, which help leaders maintain their composure and make decisions with a clear mind.

In moments of tension, leaders can also practice **forgiveness as a conscious decision**, choosing to let go of resentment or the desire for revenge. Forgiveness does not mean excusing wrongdoing, but it does involve recognizing that holding onto anger or grudges can be destructive to relationships and the overall mission. Leaders who actively practice forgiveness create an atmosphere of trust and mutual respect, encouraging collaboration and unity even in challenging times.

In conclusion, Omar ibn al-Khattab's ability to lead with forgiveness and patience offers a powerful example for modern leaders. By prioritizing reconciliation over punishment and practicing patience in moments of tension, leaders can resolve conflicts in a way that fosters peace and strengthens relationships. Forgiveness and patience are not signs of weakness in leadership but rather essential qualities that promote unity, trust, and long-term stability. Modern leaders who embrace these values will be better equipped to navigate the complexities of leadership and build more cohesive and resilient communities.

Omar's Forgiveness in Leadership: Exemplifying Patience in Difficult Situations

OMAR IBN AL-KHATTAB (may Allah be pleased with him) was renowned for his leadership marked by both strength and compassion, particularly his ability to show forgiveness in challenging situations. Despite his reputation for enforcing justice, Omar also demonstrated remarkable patience and a willingness to forgive, understanding that true leadership often requires reconciliation over retribution. His ability to balance firmness with mercy helped maintain unity within the growing Islamic state and provided an enduring example of how forgiveness can be a powerful tool in leadership.

One of the most striking examples of Omar's capacity for forgiveness occurred when a man publicly insulted him and criticized his leadership. This man expected harsh punishment, knowing that publicly challenging the caliph could lead to severe consequences. However, instead of reacting with anger or punishment, Omar chose to forgive him. Omar's response was calm, and he did not allow the insult to cloud his judgment or provoke retaliation. His forgiveness not only diffused the tension but also showed the broader community that Omar valued peace and reconciliation over personal pride or revenge. This act of patience reinforced his reputation as a fair and just leader, earning the respect of those who had witnessed the incident.

Another instance of Omar's patience and forgiveness was during his dealings with his governors and military commanders. Omar was known for holding those in positions of power accountable, but he also showed a deep understanding of the pressures they faced. In one situation, a governor made a serious error in judgment, which could have warranted his immediate dismissal. Instead of reacting impulsively, Omar took the time to understand the circumstances and forgave the governor, allowing him the opportunity to correct his mistake. Omar believed that leaders should allow room for growth and learning, recognizing that everyone, even those in leadership roles, could make mistakes. His ability to forgive in these moments helped build loyalty and trust among those who served under him.

Perhaps one of the most profound examples of Omar's forgiveness was his approach to those who had previously opposed or harmed him before his acceptance of Islam. As a former fierce opponent of Islam, Omar knew well the transformation that could come from understanding and compassion. When individuals who had once fought against him later sought his forgiveness, Omar embraced them with open arms. He did not hold their past actions against them, but instead welcomed their change of heart. This level of forgiveness extended beyond personal grudges; it was rooted in his understanding of the greater good, prioritizing unity within the Muslim community over personal vendettas.

Omar's patience was also evident in his approach to governance during crises. One notable example was during the Year of the Ashes, a time of severe famine in the Arabian Peninsula. Faced with widespread hunger and suffering, Omar showed extraordinary patience and resilience, refusing to eat anything more than the simplest food while his people starved. His patience in dealing with the crisis allowed him to make rational and compassionate decisions that prioritized the welfare of the most vulnerable. Instead of becoming overwhelmed by the enormity of the situation, Omar remained calm, patient, and focused on long-term solutions, trusting that his endurance would help guide his people through the hardship.

These stories of Omar's leadership show that his patience and forgiveness were not signs of weakness but powerful tools that strengthened his rule. His ability to forgive in difficult situations prevented conflicts from escalating and allowed for reconciliation, fostering an environment of unity and trust. Omar understood that leadership was not about asserting dominance but about guiding people with wisdom, humility, and compassion.

In conclusion, Omar ibn al-Khattab's leadership was marked by his remarkable capacity for forgiveness and patience. His ability to let go of personal grievances, show mercy to those who erred, and maintain composure in times of crisis set a powerful example of how effective leadership is built on understanding and compassion. By choosing forgiveness over retribution and practicing patience in the face of challenges, Omar strengthened the Islamic state and fostered an atmosphere of peace and unity, leaving an enduring legacy for future leaders to follow.

The Role of Forgiveness and Patience in Leadership: Key to Resolving Conflicts

FORGIVENESS AND PATIENCE are essential qualities in leadership, especially when navigating conflicts and disputes. These traits help leaders maintain harmony within their organizations, communities, and nations while promoting an atmosphere of trust and cooperation. Forgiveness allows leaders to let go of grudges and focus on solutions, while patience enables them to approach challenges with calmness and clarity. Omar ibn al-Khattab (may Allah be pleased with him) exemplified these qualities in his leadership, showing that resolving conflicts often requires understanding, compassion, and a long-term perspective. Modern leaders can learn valuable lessons from his example, especially in how to balance firmness with forgiveness and how to use patience as a strategic tool in managing disputes.

Forgiveness as a Leadership Tool

Forgiveness in leadership is not about ignoring mistakes or tolerating injustice but about recognizing that holding onto resentment can be counterproductive. Leaders who practice forgiveness create an environment where individuals are encouraged to learn from their mistakes without the fear of harsh retaliation. This promotes a culture of growth and development, where people feel supported rather than condemned.

Omar's leadership was characterized by his ability to forgive those who had wronged him, including those who had insulted or opposed him. By choosing reconciliation over punishment, he demonstrated that forgiveness can be a powerful way to build bridges and heal divisions. Leaders who can forgive show emotional intelligence, understanding that personal grudges or the desire for retribution can cloud judgment and hinder decision-making. Forgiveness also builds loyalty, as people are more likely to trust and follow a leader who shows compassion in times of conflict.

In modern leadership, forgiveness can help resolve conflicts by de-escalating tensions and fostering an atmosphere of trust. Whether in a corporate environment, political leadership, or community management, conflicts are inevitable, and leaders will often be faced with situations where forgiveness is needed to move forward. Instead of dwelling on past wrongs or mistakes, a leader who practices forgiveness can shift the focus towards problem-solving and reconciliation, encouraging others to do the same.

The Power of Patience in Conflict Resolution

Patience, like forgiveness, plays a crucial role in conflict resolution. Leaders who rush into decisions or react impulsively often exacerbate conflicts, leading to deeper divisions and longer-lasting disputes. Patience allows leaders to take the time to fully understand the complexities of a situation before acting. This thoughtful approach enables them to consider multiple perspectives, consult with advisors, and make decisions that are fair and balanced.

Omar's patience in leadership was a key factor in his ability to resolve conflicts without unnecessary escalation. He often took the time to listen to all sides of an issue before making a judgment, ensuring that his decisions were well-informed and just. This careful, measured approach earned him respect and trust from his followers, as people knew that he would not act impulsively or out of anger. In difficult situations, such as times of crisis or interpersonal disputes, Omar's patience allowed him to maintain control and find solutions that benefited the greater good.

For modern leaders, practicing patience means resisting the urge to react emotionally or immediately, especially in high-pressure situations. Leaders who cultivate patience can better manage stress and maintain clarity when facing complex challenges. Patience also creates space for reflection and collaboration, allowing leaders to involve others in the decision-making process and find solutions that are more sustainable and fair. In conflict resolution, patience enables leaders to approach disputes calmly, giving all parties the chance to express their perspectives and working towards solutions that benefit everyone involved.

Balancing Firmness with Forgiveness and Patience

While forgiveness and patience are essential, they must be balanced with firmness in leadership. Leaders must ensure that forgiveness does not come at the expense of accountability, and patience should not be confused with indecision or passivity. Omar's leadership demonstrates how these qualities can coexist. He was both firm in upholding justice and compassionate in offering forgiveness. He knew when to enforce the law and when to extend mercy, understanding that both approaches were necessary for maintaining order and unity.

Modern leaders can apply this balance by setting clear expectations and holding people accountable for their actions while also showing empathy and understanding. Forgiveness should be offered when it leads to reconciliation and growth, and patience should be exercised to avoid rash decisions that could harm long-term goals. By balancing these qualities, leaders create a leadership style that is both effective and humane.

In conclusion, forgiveness and patience are essential leadership traits, particularly in resolving conflicts. Omar ibn al-Khattab's leadership teaches us that forgiveness builds trust and fosters reconciliation, while patience allows for thoughtful, well-informed decision-making. Modern leaders can apply these lessons by promoting a culture of forgiveness and demonstrating patience in times of conflict, all while maintaining the necessary firmness to ensure justice and accountability. This balance leads to more cohesive, harmonious environments and more effective leadership overall.

Practicing Forgiveness and Striving for Reconciliation in Moments of Tension

IN MOMENTS OF TENSION and conflict, modern leaders are often faced with the difficult task of navigating disputes while maintaining harmony within their organizations or communities. Forgiveness and reconciliation are powerful tools that can help resolve conflicts, repair relationships, and foster a more collaborative environment. Leaders who practice forgiveness demonstrate emotional maturity and resilience, and by striving for reconciliation, they prioritize unity and long-term success over short-term retaliation or punishment. Omar ibn al-Khattab (may Allah be pleased with him) showed that forgiving others, even in challenging situations, can strengthen leadership and build trust. Modern leaders can apply these principles to cultivate a culture of understanding and peace.

Create a Culture of Open Communication

To practice forgiveness effectively, modern leaders must first establish an environment where open communication is encouraged. Tension often arises from misunderstandings or unresolved issues that are left unspoken. Leaders can facilitate this by creating safe spaces for dialogue, ensuring that all voices are heard and that individuals feel comfortable expressing their concerns or admitting mistakes. When people feel that they can speak openly without fear of harsh consequences, it becomes easier for forgiveness to occur, as misunderstandings are addressed early on.

By promoting active listening and empathy, leaders demonstrate that they are willing to understand others' perspectives. Omar often engaged in open dialogue with his people, listening carefully before making judgments, which helped resolve many conflicts without escalation. Modern leaders can adopt this approach by holding regular forums or meetings where concerns are discussed constructively, allowing opportunities for reconciliation.

Focus on the Bigger Picture

In moments of tension, it's important for leaders to keep the bigger picture in mind. Holding onto grudges or seeking revenge may provide temporary satisfaction, but it often undermines long-term goals and damages relationships. Forgiveness allows leaders to move past personal grievances and focus on what is best for the organization or community as a whole. Omar exemplified this by forgiving individuals who had wronged him personally, understanding that the well-being of the Muslim community was more important than his own pride.

Modern leaders can follow this example by adopting a forward-looking perspective. When faced with conflict, leaders should ask themselves how their response will affect the larger mission or vision. By prioritizing reconciliation over punishment, leaders can ensure that conflicts are resolved in a way that strengthens the group's overall cohesion and progress.

Acknowledge and Address Mistakes

Practicing forgiveness in leadership requires acknowledging that everyone, including leaders themselves, is capable of making mistakes. When leaders openly recognize their own errors, they model humility and create an atmosphere where others feel comfortable owning up to their shortcomings. This encourages a cycle of accountability and forgiveness, where mistakes are seen as opportunities for growth rather than reasons for punishment.

Leaders can demonstrate forgiveness by allowing individuals who have made mistakes to make amends and improve. Rather than dwelling on the error, leaders can help guide individuals through corrective actions, focusing on what can be learned. Omar's leadership was marked by his ability to forgive mistakes, even from high-ranking officials, and to provide opportunities for those individuals to learn and grow from their experiences. Modern leaders can apply this by practicing compassionate leadership that seeks to uplift rather than punish.

Resolve Conflicts with Patience and Empathy

Tensions often escalate when leaders react impulsively or allow emotions to guide their decisions. Patience is a key aspect of practicing forgiveness and reconciliation. It allows leaders to step back, process the situation, and approach it with a calm and thoughtful mindset. By exercising patience, leaders give themselves the time to fully understand the underlying causes of conflict and can work toward fair and constructive solutions.

Empathy is equally important in reconciliation. Leaders who empathize with those involved in a conflict are better able to mediate effectively and find common ground. Omar's ability to forgive and resolve disputes was rooted in his deep empathy for those he led, as he understood their struggles and emotions. Modern leaders can practice empathy by considering the perspectives and feelings of all parties in a conflict, allowing for more compassionate and effective resolution.

Encourage Mediation and Collaborative Problem-Solving

When conflicts arise, modern leaders can encourage mediation as a way to bring conflicting parties together. Mediation allows for a neutral third party to facilitate discussions, helping those involved to find mutually acceptable solutions. Leaders who encourage mediation show a commitment to reconciliation and emphasize the importance of dialogue over discord.

Collaborative problem-solving is another effective way to promote reconciliation. By involving all parties in finding solutions, leaders ensure that everyone feels heard and valued. This approach builds trust and reduces the likelihood of lingering resentment. Omar's leadership involved consultation and collaboration, where he sought the advice of his companions before making decisions. Modern leaders can adopt a similar approach by involving others in conflict resolution, ensuring that all voices are part of the solution.

Forgive but Maintain Accountability

Forgiveness does not mean ignoring accountability. Leaders must strike a balance between showing mercy and ensuring that individuals are held responsible for their actions. Forgiveness can be part of a constructive process where individuals are given the opportunity to make amends and improve. Omar was known for his ability to forgive while still ensuring that justice was served fairly, which strengthened trust in his leadership.

Modern leaders can practice this balance by focusing on restorative justice—seeking ways to repair harm rather than focusing solely on punishment. Forgiveness, when paired with accountability, encourages personal growth and creates a culture where individuals are empowered to learn from their mistakes while knowing they are still responsible for their actions.

In conclusion, modern leaders can practice forgiveness and strive for reconciliation by fostering open communication, focusing on long-term goals, addressing mistakes with compassion, and resolving conflicts with patience and empathy. By balancing forgiveness with accountability and encouraging collaborative problem-solving, leaders can turn moments of tension into opportunities for growth and unity. Omar ibn al-Khattab's leadership provides a timeless example of how forgiveness and patience can strengthen leadership, promote harmony, and build trust, principles that remain critical for modern leaders today.

Conclusion: The Legacy of Omar ibn al-Khattab: Timeless Lessons for Modern Leadership

Omar ibn al-Khattab (may Allah be pleased with him) remains one of history's most enduring examples of just, principled, and visionary leadership. His legacy transcends time and offers valuable lessons to modern leaders, particularly those facing today's complex political and leadership challenges. From his commitment to justice and the rule of law to his display of humility, empathy, and patience, Omar's leadership principles are as relevant today as they were during his time. He demonstrated that true leadership is not simply about power or authority but about serving others, ensuring fairness, and upholding moral integrity. Reflecting on Omar's life and governance, modern leaders can draw inspiration and guidance for navigating the ethical, social, and political landscapes they face today.

One of the most significant lessons from Omar's leadership is the importance of **justice and fairness**. His unwavering commitment to impartiality and ensuring that the law applied equally to everyone set the foundation for a just society. He never allowed personal relationships, status, or power to influence his decisions, ensuring that even his family members were not above the law. This focus on fairness created trust and stability within the Islamic state and reinforced the notion that justice is the bedrock of any healthy society. Modern leaders can apply this principle by prioritizing equality and fairness in governance, recognizing that a leader's true strength lies in their ability to uphold justice for all, regardless of social or political pressures.

Another essential takeaway from Omar's leadership is his **humility and simplicity in power**. Despite holding one of the highest positions of authority, Omar lived modestly, treating himself no differently from the people he served. He avoided the trappings of power and remained deeply connected to the concerns and struggles of the everyday people. His famous arrival in Jerusalem, dressed in simple clothes and sharing a camel with his servant, demonstrated his belief that leadership is a responsibility, not a privilege. For modern leaders, this example is a reminder that power should never distance them from the people they serve. Leaders who remain grounded, humble, and focused on service rather than personal gain are more likely to inspire loyalty and trust.

Omar's leadership was also defined by his **empathy and compassion**, especially toward the most vulnerable in society. He established social welfare systems that provided for the poor, orphans, and widows, ensuring that no one was left without support. His personal acts of charity and his concern for the well-being of all, regardless of their background or faith, exemplified his deep sense of responsibility as a leader. In an era where leaders often face stark economic disparities and social inequalities, Omar's commitment to social justice serves as a powerful model. Leaders today can learn from his example by focusing on policies that promote equity, protect the vulnerable, and build inclusive societies where everyone has access to the resources they need to thrive.

A critical aspect of Omar's leadership was his **commitment to consultation and collective wisdom**. He believed in the value of seeking advice from trusted companions before making important decisions, recognizing that leadership is strengthened by diverse perspectives. His practice of shura (consultation) demonstrated his humility and understanding that no leader, however capable, has all the answers. In today's complex and interconnected world, modern leaders can benefit from this approach by fostering open dialogue, seeking input from diverse voices, and making decisions that are informed by collective wisdom rather than individual opinion.

Omar's leadership also teaches the importance of **forgiveness and patience** in resolving conflicts. His ability to forgive those who wronged him and his willingness to show mercy in difficult situations reflected his understanding of the human condition and the need for reconciliation over retribution. His patience in leadership, particularly during crises, allowed him to make thoughtful decisions that prioritized long-term stability over immediate reactions. Modern leaders can apply these principles by approaching conflict with empathy and patience, recognizing that forgiveness can be a powerful tool for healing divisions and fostering unity.

Reflecting on **Omar's enduring influence**, his legacy continues to shape concepts of leadership, governance, and justice. He set a high standard for what it means to lead with integrity, compassion, and a deep sense of responsibility toward the well-being of society. His example serves as a guiding light for leaders across all fields—whether in politics, business, or community organizations—reminding them that effective leadership is about serving others, promoting justice, and creating lasting positive change.

The lessons from Omar's life are not bound by time or culture. His approach to leadership speaks to universal values that resonate in any era, especially in a world grappling with challenges such as inequality, injustice, and political division. **Modern leaders are called to action** by his example: to govern with justice, to lead with humility, to prioritize the needs of the vulnerable, and to embrace forgiveness and patience in the face of adversity. Omar's legacy invites today's leaders to rise to the challenge of creating a fairer, more compassionate world—one where leadership is not defined by power but by the positive impact it leaves on society.

By adopting these timeless principles, modern leaders can not only navigate the complexities of leadership but also leave a lasting legacy of their own, one that inspires future generations to lead with the same integrity, wisdom, and compassion that Omar ibn al-Khattab exemplified.

Key Lessons from Omar's Leadership for Modern Political and Leadership Challenges

OMAR IBN AL-KHATTAB (may Allah be pleased with him) left a profound legacy of leadership grounded in justice, humility, compassion, and foresight. His approach to governance and decision-making provides timeless lessons that are highly relevant to the political and leadership challenges faced today. By reflecting on his principles and actions, modern leaders can adopt strategies that promote fairness, stability, and long-term success in their communities and organizations. The following key lessons from Omar's leadership offer valuable guidance for navigating today's complex world.

The first and perhaps most important lesson from Omar's leadership is his **unwavering commitment to justice and fairness.** Omar believed that a just society could only thrive if the law was applied equally to all, regardless of status, wealth, or personal connections. He consistently demonstrated this principle by holding everyone accountable to the same legal standards, even when it involved his own family members. This impartiality built trust and stability within the Islamic state, reinforcing the idea that no one was above the law. In today's world, where issues of inequality and favoritism often erode trust in leadership, Omar's example reminds modern leaders of the importance of ensuring that justice is applied fairly and consistently, without bias or privilege.

Another essential lesson from Omar's leadership is the **value of humility and modesty in power.** Despite being one of the most powerful rulers of his time, Omar lived a life of simplicity and avoided the luxuries often associated with leadership. His modesty, both in his personal life and his public dealings, helped him stay connected to the people he served. This humility earned him the respect and loyalty of his followers, as it demonstrated that he was not leading for personal gain but for the betterment of society. In a world where many leaders become disconnected from the people they serve, Omar's humility is a reminder that true leadership is about service, not personal privilege.

Omar's leadership also highlights the importance of **empathy and compassion**, especially for the most vulnerable members of society. He implemented social welfare systems to provide for the poor, orphans, and widows, ensuring that the state supported those in need. His deep concern for justice and fairness extended beyond his own people, as he also ensured the protection and rights of non-Muslims living within the Islamic state. Modern leaders can learn from this by focusing on inclusive policies that promote social equity and protect the rights of marginalized communities. Compassionate leadership, like Omar's, fosters trust and unity, creating a society where all individuals feel valued and supported.

A critical aspect of Omar's leadership was his belief in **consultation and collective wisdom**. Before making important decisions, he sought advice and counsel from his companions, recognizing the value of diverse perspectives. This practice of consultation, known as shura, allowed Omar to make more informed decisions that reflected the needs and concerns of the wider community. For modern leaders, this lesson underscores the importance of collaboration and openness to feedback. In today's interconnected and diverse world, leaders who consult others and consider a variety of viewpoints are better equipped to make balanced and effective decisions.

Omar's **forgiveness and patience** in leadership provide another vital lesson for modern times. He understood that leadership was not about seeking revenge or punishing every mistake but about fostering reconciliation and unity. His ability to forgive those who wronged him and his patience during crises helped him maintain social harmony and prevent conflicts from escalating. Modern leaders, particularly those managing complex or divided communities, can apply this lesson by practicing forgiveness and using patience to resolve conflicts in a way that promotes healing and long-term peace.

Finally, Omar's **visionary leadership and focus on long-term sustainability** remain a critical lesson for modern leaders. He implemented administrative reforms that laid the foundation for future governance and ensured the stability of the Islamic state. His introduction of the Islamic calendar, his reorganization of the military, and his establishment of social welfare systems all reflected his forward-thinking approach. Modern leaders can learn from this by focusing not just on immediate concerns but on building systems that ensure future progress and stability. Long-term vision and strategic planning are essential for addressing today's global challenges, from climate change to economic inequality.

In conclusion, the key lessons from Omar's leadership—justice and fairness, humility in power, empathy and compassion, consultation, forgiveness and patience, and visionary leadership—offer a blueprint for effective and ethical leadership in today's world. By embracing these principles, modern leaders can navigate political and leadership challenges with integrity, ensuring that their decisions benefit both present and future generations.

Omar's Enduring Influence on Leadership, Governance, and Justice

THE LEGACY OF OMAR ibn al-Khattab (may Allah be pleased with him) continues to resonate through the ages, leaving an indelible mark on leadership, governance, and justice. His approach to ruling the Islamic state during one of its most transformative periods has set a standard for ethical, just, and effective leadership that transcends time and place. Omar's leadership model is not only celebrated in Islamic history but also admired by leaders across cultures for its profound commitment to fairness, humility, and service to the people. His influence endures because the principles he championed are timeless and universally applicable, especially in today's global context where strong, ethical leadership is more critical than ever.

Omar's impact on **leadership** is rooted in his clear sense of responsibility to the people he served. He understood leadership as a trust (amanah), where the well-being of the community was the ultimate priority. He was deeply aware that leadership was not about personal power or prestige, but about serving the needs of others with integrity and compassion. This perspective shaped his decisions and actions, setting an example for future leaders on the true meaning of servant leadership. His famous quote, "If a mule stumbles on the banks of the Euphrates, I fear that Allah will hold me accountable," reflects his sense of accountability for the welfare of even the smallest, most vulnerable creatures in his domain. Today's leaders can draw inspiration from Omar's focus on service over self-interest, understanding that true leadership is about accountability and care for all members of society, especially those most in need.

In the realm of **governance**, Omar's contributions were transformative and long-lasting. He implemented a series of administrative reforms that laid the foundation for governance in the expanding Islamic state, many of which continued to shape governance structures long after his time. One of his key reforms was the establishment of the diwan, a registry that managed the distribution of stipends and military payments, ensuring fair treatment of soldiers and public officials. This system allowed for more efficient governance and resource management, illustrating his visionary approach to statecraft. Omar also introduced the Islamic calendar, a unifying system that became a cornerstone for organizing both civic and religious life in the Muslim world. His organizational reforms ensured that the rapidly growing Islamic empire could function cohesively, even as it incorporated diverse peoples and territories. Omar's governance model, based on justice, efficiency, and foresight, offers enduring lessons for modern states seeking to balance growth with fairness and stability.

Omar's influence on **justice** is perhaps his most significant legacy. His reign is remembered as a golden era of justice, where the rule of law was upheld with absolute fairness. One of the defining aspects of his leadership was his impartial application of justice, ensuring that no one—whether a common citizen, a governor, or a member of his own family—was above the law. Omar's insistence on accountability for all, regardless of status, reinforced the idea that justice must be blind to personal connections or social rank. His dedication to justice extended beyond the Muslim community, as he ensured the protection and fair treatment of non-Muslims living under Islamic rule. This inclusivity and fairness set a powerful precedent for how justice should be administered in a diverse and pluralistic society. Today's legal and political leaders can look to Omar's example as a reminder that justice is the cornerstone of a stable and equitable society, and that leaders must be vigilant in upholding the rule of law with integrity.

Omar's legacy of justice also extends to his personal conduct as a leader. His humility and willingness to accept criticism were key elements of his just leadership. He frequently consulted with his advisors and the public, practicing shura (consultation) before making important decisions. He welcomed feedback and correction, understanding that a just leader must be open to the perspectives of others. His humility in accepting responsibility and his readiness to admit mistakes further solidified his reputation as a leader of justice. This aspect of his leadership continues to influence modern leaders, emphasizing that humility and accountability are essential qualities in the pursuit of justice.

In a world where leaders are often judged by their ability to maintain power or project strength, Omar's legacy challenges us to redefine leadership in terms of **justice, service, and humility**. His influence endures not because of his military conquests or political dominance, but because of the ethical framework he built for leadership and governance. Omar demonstrated that true leadership lies in serving others, promoting justice, and ensuring that all people—regardless of their background—are treated with fairness and respect.

Omar ibn al-Khattab's enduring legacy continues to guide and inspire leaders, scholars, and policymakers today. His principles of governance, rooted in justice, accountability, and compassion, offer a timeless model for building just societies. Modern leaders, whether in government, business, or community organizations, can learn from Omar's example that ethical leadership is not about power or control but about the well-being of the people they serve. His legacy remains a beacon of hope for those striving to lead with integrity in a world often fraught with division and inequality.

A Call to Action for Modern Leaders: Embrace the Principles of Omar ibn al-Khattab

IN A WORLD THAT IS increasingly complex, divided, and uncertain, modern leaders are faced with the daunting task of guiding their communities, organizations, and nations through unprecedented challenges. As these leaders strive to navigate issues of justice, governance, and social harmony, the timeless principles embodied by Omar ibn al-Khattab (may Allah be pleased with him) provide a roadmap for effective, ethical, and compassionate leadership. Omar's life and leadership demonstrate that true greatness lies not in the accumulation of power, but in the pursuit of justice, fairness, and service to humanity. Now, more than ever, it is crucial for modern leaders to embrace these values and integrate them into their personal and professional lives.

First and foremost, modern leaders must adopt **a steadfast commitment to justice and fairness**. In today's world, where inequality and favoritism can undermine trust in institutions, leaders who prioritize justice create societies where people feel valued and protected. Omar's unwavering dedication to the rule of law, ensuring that no one was above it, serves as a reminder that leaders must enforce laws with impartiality and fairness. Modern leaders can foster trust by building systems where accountability is universal and no one is exempt from scrutiny, regardless of their power or influence. By standing up for justice, modern leaders not only protect the integrity of their institutions but also pave the way for long-term stability and social cohesion.

Humility is another key quality that modern leaders must embrace, following the example set by Omar. **Humility in leadership is not a sign of weakness, but a source of strength**. Omar's simple lifestyle and his deep connection to the people he served earned him the respect and loyalty of those he led. Modern leaders, whether in politics, business, or social organizations, must remember that leadership is about service, not status. Humility allows leaders to stay grounded, listen to the needs of their communities, and prioritize the greater good over personal ambition. Leaders who demonstrate humility gain the trust of their followers and inspire others to work towards collective goals.

Another essential lesson from Omar's leadership that modern leaders must adopt is **empathy and compassion**. In a world rife with divisions, economic inequality, and social injustice, leaders who lead with empathy create inclusive environments where everyone is given the opportunity to succeed. Omar's care for the poor, orphans, and marginalized groups, as well as his protection of non-Muslim communities, showed that leadership is about ensuring the well-being of all, regardless of background. Modern leaders must adopt policies and practices that prioritize the most vulnerable, ensuring that resources and opportunities are distributed fairly. By leading with compassion, leaders can build societies that are stronger, more resilient, and united in their diversity.

In addition to justice, humility, and empathy, modern leaders must recognize the value of **consultation and collaboration**. Omar's practice of shura, or seeking advice and input from trusted advisors, exemplifies the importance of collective wisdom in decision-making. Modern leaders often face complex challenges that require multiple perspectives and expertise. Embracing collaboration not only leads to better-informed decisions but also fosters a sense of shared responsibility and inclusion. Leaders should build teams and systems that encourage open dialogue, transparency, and participation from diverse voices. By doing so, they create environments where innovation and problem-solving thrive.

Forgiveness and patience are also crucial leadership qualities that modern leaders must practice. The ability to forgive and exercise patience, especially in moments of tension or conflict, helps prevent escalation and promotes reconciliation. Omar's leadership was characterized by his ability to forgive those who wronged him, understanding that unity and peace were more important than personal grudges. In today's polarized world, modern leaders must rise above the impulse for retribution and instead seek common ground and peaceful resolution. Patience allows leaders to navigate crises with calmness and thoughtfulness, ensuring that decisions are made with long-term consequences in mind rather than immediate reactions.

Finally, modern leaders must have **visionary leadership** that looks beyond the present and plans for the future. Omar's reforms, from his administrative structures to the introduction of the Islamic calendar, were designed to create enduring systems that would benefit future generations. Modern leaders must also adopt a forward-thinking approach, recognizing that the decisions they make today will shape the world of tomorrow. This requires not only strategic planning but also a commitment to sustainability, inclusivity, and innovation. By focusing on long-term goals, modern leaders can leave a legacy that continues to uplift and empower future generations.

In conclusion, the principles of leadership demonstrated by Omar ibn al-Khattab—justice, humility, empathy, collaboration, forgiveness, and visionary thinking—are not just historical lessons but urgent calls to action for modern leaders. These timeless values provide the foundation for ethical leadership that prioritizes the well-being of all people and fosters a society grounded in fairness and compassion. Modern leaders, whether in government, business, or community organizations, are encouraged to reflect on these principles and actively integrate them into their leadership practices. By doing so, they can create lasting positive change, build trust, and inspire others to work towards a more just and equitable world.

Now is the time for leaders to rise to the challenge, embody the values that Omar lived by, and lead with the integrity, compassion, and vision that our world so desperately needs.

Appendix

Historical Timeline of Omar ibn al-Khattab's Life: Key Events

584 CE – **Birth of Omar ibn al-Khattab**
Omar was born in Mecca into the respected Quraysh tribe. He grew up in a noble family known for their influence in Arabian society.

616 CE – Conversion to Islam

Initially a staunch opponent of Islam, Omar's conversion marked a turning point for the early Muslim community. His strength and leadership were pivotal in defending and spreading Islam, and his conversion brought newfound confidence to Muslims who had faced persecution.

622 CE – Migration to Medina (Hijra)

Omar participated in the Hijra, the migration from Mecca to Medina, along with the Prophet Muhammad (peace be upon him) and other early Muslims. This event marked the establishment of the first Muslim community.

624 CE – Battle of Badr

Omar played an active role in the Battle of Badr, the first major battle between the Muslims and Quraysh of Mecca. The Muslim victory was significant in solidifying the strength of the early Muslim state.

625 CE – Battle of Uhud

Omar fought in the Battle of Uhud, where the Muslims faced a setback. Despite the loss, Omar's loyalty to the Prophet and the Muslim cause remained steadfast.

627 CE – Battle of the Trench (Khandaq)

Omar participated in the defense of Medina during the Battle of the Trench, where the Muslims successfully resisted a large Quraysh siege.

632 CE – Death of the Prophet Muhammad (peace be upon him)

The Prophet Muhammad's passing was a profound moment for the Muslim community. Omar, who had been one of the Prophet's closest companions, initially struggled to accept the Prophet's death before being comforted by Abu Bakr's famous speech.

632 CE – Omar's Role in Abu Bakr's Caliphate

After the death of the Prophet, Omar played a crucial role in securing the election of Abu Bakr as the first caliph (successor). Omar was one of Abu Bakr's key advisors during his short reign.

634 CE – Omar Becomes the Second Caliph

After Abu Bakr's death, Omar was elected the second caliph of the Rashidun Caliphate. His reign marked one of the most significant periods of expansion and reform in Islamic history.

634-644 CE – Omar's Caliphate: Territorial Expansion

Under Omar's leadership, the Islamic empire expanded rapidly. Key conquests included Syria, Iraq, Palestine, Egypt, and parts of Persia. These conquests were not only military victories but also laid the groundwork for the Islamic world's cultural and political development.

636 CE – Battle of Yarmouk

The Muslim army, under Khalid ibn al-Walid's command, defeated the Byzantine Empire in the Battle of Yarmouk, a pivotal event that solidified Muslim control of Syria. Omar played a strategic role in this campaign.

638 CE – Conquest of Jerusalem

Omar's conquest of Jerusalem was significant not just for its military importance but for his humane treatment of the city's inhabitants. Omar ensured the protection of Christian sites, and his entry into Jerusalem is remembered for its simplicity and humility.

638 CE – Introduction of the Islamic Calendar

Omar formalized the Islamic (Hijri) calendar, which began with the Prophet's migration to Medina. This calendar remains in use today for Islamic religious observances.

639 CE – Plague of Amwas

A devastating plague struck the region of Syria and Palestine, killing thousands, including some of Omar's closest commanders. Omar's leadership during the crisis was characterized by compassion and his concern for the welfare of his people.

644 CE – Assassination of Omar ibn al-Khattab

Omar was assassinated while leading the Fajr prayer in Medina by a Persian slave named Abu Lu'lu'a. His assassination marked the end of one of the most significant eras in Islamic history.

644 CE – Burial of Omar ibn al-Khattab

Omar was buried alongside the Prophet Muhammad (peace be upon him) and Abu Bakr in the Prophet's Mosque in Medina. His legacy as a just, humble, and visionary leader continues to be celebrated throughout the Muslim world.

Additional Resources: Further Reading on Omar's Leadership and Islamic History

FOR READERS WHO WISH to delve deeper into the life of Omar ibn al-Khattab and the broader context of early Islamic history, the following books, articles, and resources provide insightful perspectives on his leadership, governance, and the Islamic world during his time.

176

1. Books on Omar ibn al-Khattab and Early Islamic History:

○ **"Omar Ibn Al-Khattab: His Life and Times" by Ali M. Sallabi**

This comprehensive biography offers an in-depth look at Omar's life, focusing on his contributions as the second caliph, his personal qualities, and his impact on the Muslim world. It provides valuable historical context and highlights Omar's leadership style.

○ **"The Rightly Guided Caliphs" by Abul Hasan Ali Nadwi**

This book covers the lives of the four Rashidun caliphs, including Omar, emphasizing their leadership and contributions to Islamic governance. It offers a concise yet insightful account of their reigns and the political and social developments that shaped early Islam.

○ **"The Life of the Prophet Muhammad (4 Volumes)" by Ibn Kathir**

Although focused on the Prophet Muhammad (peace be upon him), this classic work contains important references to Omar's role as a companion and leader. It provides a comprehensive account of early Islamic history and offers context for Omar's rise to leadership.

○ **"Al-Farooq: The Life of Omar the Great" by Shibli Nomani**

A well-regarded biography that explores the life and character of Omar ibn al-Khattab, emphasizing his role as a reformer and statesman. The book delves into the administrative reforms he implemented and his influence on Islamic governance.

o **"Lost Islamic History: Reclaiming Muslim Civilisation from the Past" by Firas Alkhateeb**

This accessible book provides a broader history of the Islamic world, including the Rashidun period. It helps readers understand the significance of Omar's contributions within the larger context of Islamic civilization.

2. Articles and Journals:

o **"Omar ibn al-Khattab and His Impact on the Early Islamic State"** – Available in various Islamic studies journals, this article offers a scholarly exploration of Omar's political and social reforms, particularly his role in shaping Islamic governance.

o **"The Just Caliphs: Leadership in Islam"** – This article, published in academic journals on leadership and Islamic studies, focuses on the concept of leadership in Islam, using the Rashidun caliphs, including Omar, as models of just and ethical leadership.

o **"The Conquests of Omar: A Turning Point in Islamic History"** – A detailed examination of Omar's military campaigns and territorial expansions, analyzing their significance for the Islamic world and the political landscape of the time.

○ **"The Role of Shura in Omar's Leadership"** – This article highlights Omar's use of consultation (shura) in decision-making, exploring how his collaborative leadership style influenced Islamic governance and set a precedent for future rulers.

3. Websites and Online Resources:

○ **Al-Islam.org**

This website offers a wealth of resources on Islamic history, including articles and multimedia presentations on the Rashidun caliphs, with a focus on Omar's leadership. It provides both historical overviews and detailed studies on various aspects of his caliphate.

○ **The Seerah Foundation**

A comprehensive source for biographical information on key figures in Islamic history, including the Rightly Guided Caliphs. The website features articles, lectures, and podcasts on the life and legacy of Omar ibn al-Khattab.

○ **Kalamullah.com – The History of the Caliphs**

This resource provides access to books, articles, and other educational materials focused on the Rashidun caliphate, including Omar's time as caliph. It is a helpful platform for those seeking historical texts and Islamic leadership principles.

○ **Yaqeen Institute for Islamic Research**

Yaqeen Institute offers scholarly articles and research papers on Islamic history and leadership. Several of their publications explore the role of justice, governance, and leadership in Islam, with references to Omar's caliphate.

4. Documentaries and Lectures:

○ **"The Life of Omar ibn al-Khattab" – Islamic History Series**

This documentary series, available on platforms such as YouTube, provides a detailed account of Omar's life, his rise to leadership, and his contributions to the expansion and governance of the early Islamic state.

○ **Sheikh Yasir Qadhi's Lecture Series on the Rightly Guided Caliphs**

Sheikh Yasir Qadhi, a prominent Islamic scholar, offers a comprehensive lecture series that covers the lives of the four Rightly Guided Caliphs. His lectures on Omar focus on his leadership style, his contributions to Islamic governance, and the lessons modern leaders can learn from him.

○ **"Omar Ibn Al-Khattab" TV Series**

This historical drama series, available on several streaming platforms, provides a dramatized depiction of Omar's life, leadership, and the key events of his time. It offers a visual understanding of his legacy, making it accessible for those new to Islamic history.

These resources provide a diverse array of insights into Omar ibn al-Khattab's leadership and the broader historical context of early

Islam. Whether you're seeking academic research, historical narratives, or practical lessons for leadership, these materials will deepen your understanding of one of history's greatest leaders and the foundational period of Islamic governance.

human connection. If you're ready to inspire real change and create lasting impact, this book is your essential guide.

—Jeannie Jones-Ledford, CEO of J3

A powerful and deeply resonant exploration of what it truly means to lead with authenticity. Carole Adolphe's journey—from a focus on process, performance, and deadlines to a grounded, self-aware, and purpose-driven approach—reminds us that leadership is not defined by title or hierarchy, but by mindset and intention.

This book demonstrates the transformative impact of pausing, becoming present, and leading from clarity rather than pressure. Through compelling examples, it shows how authenticity builds trust, transparency fosters compassion, and vision inspires others. *Permission to Lead Differently* is an important guide for leaders seeking to realign their work with who they truly are.

—Karen Metzler, Senior Executive